AF254359

The Complete Car Sales Survival Guide

The No-BS Playbook for New Automotive Salespeople

Bruce Huddleston

Bedrock Heritage Publishing

Published by:

Bedrock Heritage Publishing

A Division of Life Guidance Consulting LLC

Tyler, Texas

www.bedrockheritagepublishing.com

info@bedrockheritagepublishing.com

ISBN: 978-1-972179-41-3 (Paperback)

ISBN: 978-1-972179-42-0 (eBook / EPUB)

Library of Congress Control Number: 2026910705

First Edition, 2026

Printed in the United States of America

Also By Bruce Huddleston

Disclaimer

This book is based on the author's personal and professional experiences, observations, and opinions, accumulated over a 35-year career in the automotive industry. It is intended for educational and informational purposes only.

The stories, anecdotes, and examples contained in this book are drawn from real-world situations encountered throughout the author's career. However, names, identifying details, specific circumstances, employer names, dealership names, and individual characteristics have been changed, omitted, combined, or fictionalized to protect the privacy of the individuals involved. Any resemblance to specific living persons, current or former employers, or existing businesses is coincidental and unintentional.

No individual, dealership, organization, or employer referenced or implied in the stories within this book has reviewed, approved, or endorsed the content herein. The recollections and characterizations presented are solely the author's own perspective and memory of events and do not constitute a factual record, legal testimony, or statement of fact regarding any identifiable person or entity.

The sales strategies, techniques, scripts, and professional advice presented in this book reflect the author's personal approach and experience. Individual results in automotive sales will vary based on experience, effort, market conditions, dealership policies, and other factors beyond the author's control. Nothing in this book constitutes a guarantee of income, employment, or professional outcome.

References to third-party companies, software platforms, CRM tools, training programs, industry organizations, and trademarked products are made for informational and educational purposes only. Such references do not constitute endorsement by or affiliation with those companies, nor do those companies endorse or sponsor this publication. All trademarks and registered trademarks are the property of their respective owners.

The author and publisher have made reasonable efforts to ensure the accuracy of information presented in this book at the time of writing. However, the automotive industry, technology, and business practices change rapidly. The author and publisher make no representations or warranties regarding the completeness, accuracy, or current applicability of the information contained herein, and expressly disclaim any liability arising from the use or application of the content of this book.

This book is sold with the understanding that the author and publisher are not engaged in rendering legal, financial, tax, or other professional advice. Readers with specific professional questions are encouraged to consult qualified professionals in the relevant field.

By reading this book, you acknowledge and agree that the author and publisher shall not be liable for any damages, losses, or claims arising directly or indirectly from the use of or reliance upon any information contained herein.

SPECIAL SALES AND BULK ORDERS

Special discounts are available for dealerships, sales organizations, training programs, and educational institutions purchasing this book or The Car Sales Survival Series in quantity. For bulk order pricing and custom packages, contact:

info@bedrockheritagepublishing.com

www.bedrockheritagepublishing.com

Free Bonus for Readers

Your Complete Digital Script Library

As a reader of The Complete Car Sales Survival Guide, you have access to the complete digital version of every script in this book, formatted, printable, and ready to customize in your own voice.

To access the full library, go to:

www.carsalessurvivalseries.com/scripts

The Complete Phone Script Library

All 8 scripts from the Appendix in digital, editable format

Additional Objection Handling Scenarios

Expanded responses beyond what fit in this book

Updates as the Industry Evolves

New scripts and resources, as AI and digital tools change the business

Access to the Full Car Sales Survival Series

Browse and order all micro books from the series

www.bedrockheritagepublishing.com

Contents

INTRODUCTION

And Why This Book Is Different From Every Other Sales Book You've Seen

My grandfather was a salesman. He worked in outside sales, selling tool and die equipment, grinding wheels, drill bits, the kind of stuff that keeps factories running.

When I was ten or eleven, he used to take me along on his summer visits to customers. I'd ride with him, watch him walk into a shop, shake hands with the guys on the floor, and walk out with an order.

That's where it started. A kid watching his grandfather work a room and thinking: I want to do that someday.

It took me a while to get there.

By the time I was seventeen, I'd gotten a girl pregnant, done the right thing and married her, and gone to work in a machine shop to support my family—no high school diploma. No college. Just a young man with a wife, a baby, and a job that paid the bills. When that marriage didn't survive, and young marriages under that kind of pressure often don't, I kept working the machines. It was steady. It was honest. And I was absolutely miserable.

What I really wanted was to be in sales.

Eventually, I made the decision that changed everything. I left Texas, moved to Oregon, and walked into the first dealership I could find. Then the second. Both turned me away. Didn't like how I was dressed. Not polished enough. Not the right look for their showroom floor.

The third place I tried was a Dodge dealership. They hired me.

On my first day on the job, my new sales manager looked me over and asked for my name.

"Bruce," I said.

"What's your middle name?"

"Edward."

He nodded. "We already got a Bruce. From here on out, you're Ed. Does that work for you?"

I thought about it for about half a second. I needed the job. And honestly, being single with an alias wasn't the worst situation in the world.

"Sure," I said. "I can be Ed."

I worked for that same dealership for 25 years. Within a few years of being hired by the man who named me Ed, I became his boss. We're still good friends to this day.

That's the short version of how I got into the car business. The longer version involves thirty-five years of selling cars, managing sales floors, running used car operations, working a decade in buy here pay here as finance manager, sales manager, and general manager, and eventually retiring at sixty-four with a home, money in the bank, a life coaching practice, and a publishing business.

I am not rich. I want to be clear about that. I live in an average house in Texas. But I have no debt, a wife who loves and supports me, and a career that gave me more than most people ever get from any job: the real knowledge of how to deal with people.

I'm telling you all of this because I want you to understand who this book is from. It's not from a consultant who studied the car business from the outside. It's not from a corporate trainer who memorized someone else's program. It's from a high school dropout who figured this business out the hard way, worked every level of it, and wants to give you the education he never got when he walked onto that lot for the first time.

What This Book Is

This is a survival guide. The title says it plainly: The Complete Car Sales Survival Guide.

Not a motivational book. Not a theory book. Not a book full of charts and frameworks invented by people who never sold a car in their lives. This is the book I wish someone had handed me on day one.

It covers the seven steps of a sale, the same basic process used in every dealership in the country, but shows how they actually work in the real world, not how a corporate training video presents them. It covers the psychology of customers, because understanding how people think is more valuable than any script you'll ever memorize. It covers the mistakes that cost new salespeople their confidence and their commissions. And it covers all of this through real stories, because real stories are how people actually learn.

Some of those stories are funny. Some of them are painful. All of them contain a lesson that I learned the hard way,

So you don't have to.

What This Book Is Not

This is not a book that tells you selling is easy. It isn't.

This is not a book that promises you'll be closing deals within your first week. You probably won't.

This is not a book that sugarcoats the car business.

The car business can be brutal. The hours are long. The culture can be cutthroat. At most dealerships, the "training" amounts to someone pointing at the lot and saying, "Go talk to people."

If that's what you're walking into, this book is designed to give you what they didn't.

Who This Book Is For

This book is for anyone new to the car business or thinking about getting into it.

It's for the person who just got hired and doesn't know where to start. It's for the person who's been on the floor for six months and can't figure out why the process keeps breaking down. It's for the person who's been told to shadow an experienced salesperson and has figured out pretty quickly that the experienced salesperson has zero interest in training them.

It's also for people who have never considered car sales before but are wondering if it's something they could do. The answer, by the way, is probably yes. The car business is one of the few industries left where you need no degree, your income has no ceiling, and the only thing standing between where you are and where you want to be is the willingness to learn and work harder than the person next to you.

I know that's true because I'm living proof of it.

How to Use This Book

Read it straight through the first time. The seven steps of a sale build on each other, and understanding how they connect matters as much as understanding each one individually. Think of it like the waltz analogy I'll give you later: you can't pick and choose which steps to do. The sequence is the system.

After that, use it as a reference. Come back to the chapter on closing when you keep losing deals at the end. Come back to the chapter on the four types of buyers when a negotiation stops making sense. Come back to the stories when you need to be reminded that every veteran in this business has a collection of moments that went sideways and that they survived.

The goal is simple: help you survive your first year in this business, make enough money that staying is worth it, and build the kind of career that, thirty-five years later, you're proud of.

Let's get started.

"The Rule: The car business will give you everything you're willing to earn. It won't give you anything you're not."

CHAPTER 1

THE REALITY OF THE CAR BUSINESS

WHAT THEY DON'T TELL You Before You Start

Most people who walk into the car business for the first time have a picture in their head of what it will look like.

They imagine standing on a nice, clean lot, greeting customers, showing them a few cars, writing up some paperwork, and collecting a commission check. Straightforward. Pleasant, even. A customer comes in, you help them find something they like, everybody shakes hands, and you go home with money in your pocket.

That's the picture. And it's not entirely wrong. That does happen. It just doesn't happen the way most new people imagine it will.

What they don't see is that, before they start, nobody tells them about everything else.

The Hours

The car business does not run on a nine-to-five schedule. Most dealerships are open six or seven days a week. Evenings are often the busiest time because that's when people are off work and ready to shop. Weekends are prime time. Holidays can go either way, dead slow or unexpectedly busy, and you rarely know which until you're standing there in it.

This means your schedule will look nothing like the schedules of most people you know. When your friends are at a cookout on Saturday afternoon, you're on the lot. When your family is watching football on Sunday, you might be doing a delivery. When a deal comes together at 7:30 in the evening, you stay until it's done.

That's the reality. If you go in knowing it, you can plan for it. If you go in expecting something different, it will grind you down fast.

The Emotional Roller Coaster

I want you to imagine this. You spent three hours with a customer—good conversation, solid test drive, numbers that made sense. You're feeling confident. And then they look at you and say, "We need to go home and think about it."

In thirty-five years, I heard that sentence more times than I can count. And every single time, for most salespeople, it feels like a punch in the stomach.

One minute you're celebrating a deal in your head. The next minute, you're standing on the lot, wondering what the hell just happened.

That swing from high to low, sometimes multiple times in a single day, is one of the things nobody prepares new salespeople for. And it breaks a lot of them. Not because they aren't capable, but because they don't understand yet that this is just part of the business. The ones who survive learn to stay steady. They treat every customer as a fresh opportunity, regardless of what the last one did.

Easier said than done. But it can be learned.

The Training Or Lack of It

Here's one of the honest truths about this industry that most people find out the hard way: most dealerships do not train their salespeople.

Oh, they'll say they do. They'll assign you a mentor or tell you to shadow an experienced salesperson. What they don't tell you is that the person you're shadowing has no real incentive to teach you anything. You're not their problem. Worse, you're future competition. If you learn to sell, you'll be taking deals that might have gone to them.

So what happens? You become the gopher. You move cars, you get lunches, you watch deals happen around you without anyone explaining what's actually going on or why. You learn by making mistakes, and you make a lot of them.

I know because that's exactly what happened to me. I walked onto that Dodge lot in the late eighties with no training manual, no videos, no computer system, and no real guidance. We tracked our customers with index cards. Literally a small card with the customer's name, phone number, date of birth, spouse's name, kids' names, whatever we could collect. That was our CRM. The whole relationship lived on a 3x5 card in a little box on your desk.

There were no cell phones. No internet. Customers couldn't look up invoice pricing before they walked in. They couldn't compare our prices to the dealership across town without actually driving across town; in some ways, that made the job simpler. In other ways, particularly the part where you were learning on your own through trial and painful error, it was brutal.

That world is gone now. But the sink-or-swim training culture at a lot of dealerships? That's still very much alive.

Which is exactly why this book exists.

What the Good Days Look Like

I don't want to paint the picture too dark, because the flip side is real too.

When this business is good, it's very good.

There are days when you sell three cars before noon. There are months when your commission check makes you feel like you're printing money. There are moments, and any salesperson who's been in this long enough will tell you the same thing, where everything just clicks. You connect with a customer immediately. The car is right. The numbers work. The deal flows from start to finish as it should. You hand someone the keys to something they're genuinely excited about, and you made that happen.

That feeling doesn't get old.

And unlike almost any other job I can think of, the car business rewards effort directly. You are, in almost every sense, self-employed. The dealership provides the roof, the inventory, and the tools. What you do with that is entirely up to you. Nobody is going to cap your income. Nobody is going to tell you that you've sold enough this month. The ceiling is as high as you're willing to go.

I've seen salespeople in this business make extraordinary livings. I've also seen people walk away after sixty days because they weren't willing to put in what it takes. The difference between those two groups is rarely talent. It's almost always commitment.

The One Thing That Separates the Survivors From Everyone Else

Early in my career, I watched salespeople come and go constantly. The lot was a revolving door. Someone new would show up, get a little training, struggle through a few weeks, and disappear. Then someone else would take their spot and do the same thing.

The ones who stayed, the ones who were still there a year later, five years later, twenty years later, had one thing in common. It wasn't charisma. It wasn't product knowledge. It wasn't even natural talent with people.

It was tenacity.

They showed up. They kept showing up. They didn't badmouth the dealership when things were slow. They didn't take it personally when a deal fell apart. They didn't quit after a bad week. They learned from what went wrong and came back the next day ready to try again.

I know this because it's how I survived my own early years. I wasn't the most naturally gifted salesperson on the floor. I struggled with scripts. I was terrified to ask for the sale. I froze up at the wrong moments. But I worked longer hours than most people around me, I stayed positive when others were complaining, and I committed fully committed to learning how to do the job right.

Eventually, that commitment became competence. And competence became confidence. And confidence became a career.

That's the path. It's not glamorous. It's not fast. But it works.

A Word About This Business and Money

Before we go any further, I want to say something about money that most books in this space won't say out loud.

The car business can pay you very well. It can also fool you into spending everything you make and then some, because when the commissions are coming in, it feels like they always will. They don't.

This business has peaks and valleys. February is often a great month because tax returns hit, and people buy cars. January can be brutally slow. Christmas week is unpredictable. Summer can be strong. There will be months when you feel like you can't make a wrong move, and months when you wonder if you've forgotten how to do the job.

The salespeople who thrive long-term are the ones who learn to manage their income like a business owner, not like someone with a guaranteed paycheck. Know what you need every month to cover your life. When the big months come, bank the difference. Don't let a great February turn into a crisis in March.

We'll talk more about this later. For now, just know it's part of the reality nobody tells you upfront.

What Comes Next

The rest of this book is built around a system. Seven steps that successful salespeople move through with every customer, in a specific sequence, for specific reasons.

Before we get into the steps, there are a few more things you need to understand about the business itself, the psychology of customers, the types of buyers you'll encounter, and why the culture of the car business is the way it is. All of that comes in the next few chapters.

But if you take nothing else from this first chapter, take this:

"The Rule: The car business is not what you expect. It is harder than it looks, more rewarding than most people realize, and completely worth it if you're willing to do what it takes. The question is whether you are."

CHAPTER 2

BEFORE YOU WALK OUT THAT DOOR

Managing Yourself, Your Money, and Your Time in a Business That Runs on Neither

Nobody tells you this before you start, so I'm going to tell you now.

The car business is commission-based. That means your income will swing. There will be months when you feel like you're printing money, and months when you're staring at your bills, wondering how you're going to make them work. Both of those experiences are completely normal. What separates the people who build real careers in this business from those who burn out and leave is understanding that those swings are coming and planning for them before they arrive.

Most new salespeople don't do this. They have a great February, spend like it's going to last forever, and then hit a slow March completely unprepared. Then they get stressed. Then they get desperate. And a desperate salesperson is a bad salesperson, because desperation is something customers can feel the moment you walk up to them.

So before we get into the steps of the sale, before we talk about meet and greets and test drives and closing, we need to talk about the thing that's going to keep you in the game long enough to get good at all of it.

Know Your Number

The first thing I want you to do before your first paycheck, if possible, is sit down and figure out what it costs you to live every month. Rent or mortgage. Car payment. Insurance. Food. Utilities. Everything. Add it up and write it down.

That number is your floor. That's the minimum you need to bring home every single month, no matter what.

Now here's the discipline part. When you have a big month, and your commission check comes in well above that floor, you do not spend the difference. You bank it. Every dollar above what you need to live goes into a reserve account and stays there until you need it.

Because you will need it. Maybe not next month. But eventually, the lot will go quiet. Maybe it's January. Maybe it's a weird stretch in the summer when nobody seems to be buying. Maybe it's a personal situation. Whatever it is, that reserve is what keeps you from making decisions out of panic.

A simple rule of thumb: when you have a great month, reward yourself with ten or fifteen percent of the overage. Take your family to dinner. Buy yourself something you've been wanting. You earned it. Then bank the rest.

That discipline, more than any sales technique I can teach you, is what will allow you to stay in this business long enough to get really good at it.

Know Your Calendar

The car business has seasons, and if you pay attention, you can plan around them.

February is often one of the strongest months of the year. Tax returns start hitting, and people buy cars. If you're going to have a great month, February is a good bet. Work it hard.

January, on the other hand, is frequently slow. People just spent money on Christmas. Their credit cards are high. They're not thinking about a car payment. Expect January to be lean and budget accordingly.

The stretch right after Christmas and into New Year's can go either way. Sometimes it's dead. Sometimes it's surprisingly busy because people are off work, bored, and have gift money to spend. You won't know until you're in it, which is why the reserve matters.

Summers can be strong, particularly for trucks and SUVs. Back-to-school season can move smaller vehicles. The end of the month is almost always more productive than the beginning because managers are pushing to hit their numbers, and deals that wouldn't have gotten approved on the fifth of the month might sail through on the twenty-ninth.

Learn these rhythms. Work hard when the business is there. And for the love of everything, take your vacation in January, not in February.

Know Your Schedule

This sounds obvious, but I've watched more salespeople undermine themselves with their own schedules than almost anything else.

If your dealership is open on Saturdays, you need to be there. Saturday is often the highest traffic day of the week. Missing it because you want a weekend like the rest of the world is costing you deals. The dealership isn't going to close on Saturday for you. The customers are going to come. The only question is whether you're there to help them or someone else is.

Evenings matter too. Plenty of buyers can only shop after work. If you duck out early because it's been a slow afternoon, you're potentially walking out the door right before your best opportunity of the day walks in.

Be there. Be ready. Be consistent.

The Pilot Analogy

I want to give you an analogy I've used in training for years because it puts the consistency piece into perspective.

Imagine you're boarding an airplane. The pilot comes over the intercom before takeoff and says, "Good morning, folks. Just want to let you know, I'm a pretty good pilot. I land this plane successfully about ninety-five percent of the time. Should be a great flight."

You're off that plane. Immediately. Every single one of us is off that plane.

Ninety-five percent isn't good enough when the stakes are that high. You want a pilot who lands the plane 100% of the time. You want a pilot who follows the checklist every single flight, not just when they feel like it.

Sales is the same way. The steps of this process serve a purpose. They work when they're followed. They don't work when you decide to skip the ones that feel unnecessary or slow. A salesperson who follows the process 90% of the time will achieve 90% of the results at best. The ones at the top of the board do it right 100% of the time.

Consistency is the skill. Everything else flows from it.

The Sock Analogy

Here's a simpler version of the same idea.

I'll bet you get dressed the same way every morning. Left sock first, or right whichever it is, I'd bet you do it the same way every day without thinking about it. You put your clothes on in the same order. You run through the same routine. It's so automatic you don't even notice anymore.

Try doing it backward sometimes. Reverse your whole routine. It's cumbersome. You feel off. Things don't flow the way they're supposed to.

That's what happens when you do the steps of a sale out of order or skip one entirely. The whole thing gets cumbersome. Things don't flow. And customers feel that even if they can't name it.

Do it the same way every time, in the right sequence, and it becomes automatic. And when it becomes automatic, it becomes natural. And when it becomes natural, it starts working.

FROM THE FLOOR

Early in my career, I had a stretch of bad months in a row. Not because the lot was slow. Because I was spending everything I made the moment I made it. Good week? Great dinner. Good month? New clothes, new stuff, nights out. I felt like I was doing well because the money was coming in.

Then I hit a slow stretch. And I had nothing: no reserve, no cushion, nothing to fall back on. I was stressed every single day, which made me desperate, which pushed me to work customers too hard, which made my numbers worse. It was a cycle that almost pushed me out of the business entirely.

What saved me was simple: I started treating my commissions like a business owner treats revenue, not like an employee treats a paycheck. I figured out my floor, I built a reserve, and I never let myself get caught like that again.

The car business will give you the income to do this right. Don't let it fool you into spending your way into a crisis.

"The Rule: Manage your money before it manages you. Know your floor, bank the difference, and take your vacation in January."

CHAPTER 3

THE DISNEYLAND PRINCIPLE

WHY YOU'RE ALWAYS ON Stage, Whether You Know It or Not

Have you ever thought about how Disneyland actually works? Not the rides. Not the food. The operation. The way the whole place stays "magic" even when there are thousands of people moving through it every day, even when it's a hundred degrees in July, even when things go wrong behind the scenes.

Part of the answer is that the park has two tiers. There's the park itself, the streets, the rides, and the characters walking around making kids' days. And then there's an entire underground network beneath it: tunnels, break rooms, staging areas, service corridors. That's where Mickey Mouse eats his lunch. That's where Goofy takes off his head and has a cup of coffee between appearances. That's where the real world lives.

But the moment those characters step up through that door and into the park, something switches. They're not employees on a break anymore. They're performers. They're on stage. And while they're on stage, the mask never slips. Not for fatigue, not for a bad day, not for a difficult guest. The character stays in character because that's the job.

We need to operate the same way.

The Moment You Step Onto the Lot

Your break room is your break room. Your car in the parking lot is your car. The back office, the lunch table, the smoking area out back, those are your underground tunnels. That's where you get to be off. Where you can complain about a rough morning, laugh at something dumb that happened, and decompress between customers. That's fine. That's human.

But the moment you step onto that showroom floor or out onto that lot, you're in the park. You're on stage. And the performance standard changes completely.

No eye rolls when a customer asks a question you've answered a hundred times. No sighing when it's raining, and you have to go outside. No side conversations with coworkers while a customer is trying to get someone's attention. No visible irritation, no bad energy, no "I'm having a terrible day" leaking through your expression.

You are the professional. The customer doesn't care about your morning. They care about their car.

Attitude Is Visible

I want to be direct with you about something: customers can read you. Not perfectly, not always consciously, but they can feel your energy within seconds of seeing you. And that energy, whether it's genuine enthusiasm or barely concealed indifference, shapes everything that follows.

I've watched salespeople lose deals before they ever said a word. They'd be standing on the lot looking like they'd rather be anywhere else, and a customer would pull in, look at them for two seconds, and drive right back out. Not because the price was wrong. Not because the inventory wasn't right. Because the person standing there didn't look like someone they wanted to spend the next two hours with.

On the other side, I've watched salespeople with average product knowledge and average closing skills outsell everyone around them simply because they showed up with the right energy every single day. They were genuinely happy to see customers. Not fake happy, genuinely. They treated every person who came onto that lot like they were the most interesting thing that had happened all day.

That attitude is a choice. It's something you decide to bring before you walk out the door.

FROM THE FLOOR

I worked with a saleswoman who came in one morning after a fight with her husband. The argument was the classic one: who would take the kids to the doctor? He thought his job was more important. She thought hers was. Neither one was exactly wrong, but neither was backing down either.

She came in anyway. And here's the thing, she had good reason to. She had an appointment that day with a customer who wanted to purchase two vehicles. Not one. Two. Any salesperson who has been around long enough knows what that means. An appointment already has a higher closing ratio than a fresh up off the lot. An appointment for two vehicles at nearly fifty thousand dollars total is the kind of morning that can carry your whole week.

She wasn't going to miss it.

But she wasn't there. Not mentally. She was still in that argument, still running the morning through her head, still carrying everything she hadn't been able to say before she walked out the door. Her mind was at home with her kids and her husband, while her body was on the sales floor.

It showed. She was distracted. Unfocused. She made errors, pulled around the wrong vehicle at one point, lost the thread of the conversation with the customer, and missed the signals that would have told her where they were in the process. And somewhere in that interaction, the customer's confidence in her began to slip.

When the customer loses confidence in the salesperson, they lose confidence in the dealership. That's how it works. The two things are connected.

The appointment fell apart. Both vehicles. Nearly fifty thousand dollars in sales walked out the door.

She lost two commissions. The desk lost the profit on two deals. The finance manager lost his back-end income. The dealership lost a customer who came in ready to buy.

And her husband still had to take the kids to the doctor.

Nobody won that day. Not because she wasn't capable, she absolutely was. But because she stepped onto the stage without being ready to perform. The customer felt it before she ever realized what was happening.

You don't always get to control what happens before you walk in. But you do get to control what happens the moment you step onto that lot. Leave it in the car. Leave it in the parking lot. Leave it in whatever tunnel is yours. Because the moment you walk through that door, you owe the customer and yourself your full attention.

What "On Stage" Actually Means

Being on stage doesn't mean being fake. In fact, fake is the one thing that will undermine you faster than anything else. Customers have finely tuned radar for insincerity. They've dealt with too many salespeople who were all smiles until the deal fell apart.

What it means is that you're intentional. You've made a decision, before you walked out that door, about how you're going to show up. Not reactive, intentional. Your mood doesn't get to run the floor. The customer's experience does.

It means you're dressed appropriately for your workplace. Not every dealership requires a suit and tie; in fact, walking into a buy here, pay here lot in a three-piece suit might actually work against you, because it creates distance between you and your customer. But clean, professional, and appropriate for your environment? Always. Whatever the dress code is, exceed it slightly. You want to look like someone who takes the job seriously.

It means you're aware. You know what's coming onto the lot. You know which cars are where. You know your inventory. You're not caught off guard when a customer asks about a specific vehicle because you walked the lot that morning.

And it means you're consistent. Not just on your good days. Every day.

The Lot Is a Stage, and You're Always Being Watched

Here's something most new salespeople don't fully grasp: customers who haven't even gotten out of their car yet are already watching you.

They pull into the lot, sit in their car for a moment to gather their thoughts, and look around. They're watching the salespeople. They're deciding who looks approachable. They're deciding whether they feel comfortable enough to get out.

If you're standing on the lot looking sharp, aware, and ready, not staring them down, but present and professional, they're more likely to step out. If you're slumped against a car scrolling your phone, looking like you'd rather be anywhere else, some of them won't bother. They'll just leave.

Now, not every customer who leaves does so because of the sales staff. Sometimes they don't see a vehicle they like. Sometimes they're just browsing. That's part of the business.

But don't ignore what you can control. I've seen it happen. Cars pull in, take a slow loop around the lot, and leave without anyone ever stepping out. And in many cases, the way the sales floor looks and feels plays a role in that decision.

You are the first thing the customer evaluates. Make sure you're worth evaluating.

One More Thing About the Disneyland Principle

Mickey Mouse doesn't argue with guests. He doesn't get into it with rude kids. He doesn't snap at someone who bumps into him. He stays in character because the character is bigger than any single moment.

You're going to deal with difficult customers. You're going to deal with rude people, people who waste your time, people who negotiate in bad faith, people who are just having a miserable day and taking it out on whoever is in front of them.

Stay in character.

Don't argue back. Don't get sarcastic. Don't let someone else's bad day become your bad performance. If the situation escalates to the point where you can't recover it professionally, you get a manager. That's what managers are for. But you do not go to war with a customer on a dealership lot. That's a scene, and scenes cost you deals not just with that customer, but with everyone who witnesses it.

Be the professional in the room. Always.

"The Rule: The moment you step onto that lot, you're on stage. The character you play is the best version of yourself. Stay in character."

CHAPTER 4

DANCING THE WALTZ

THE SEVEN STEPS OF a Sale and Why the Sequence Is Everything

I want you to picture a waltz.

It's a specific dance. It has specific steps. Those steps go in a specific order, and they connect in a specific way. If you follow them correctly, the whole thing flows. It looks effortless. It's actually quite beautiful when it's done right.

Now imagine someone doing the waltz but deciding, halfway through, that they don't feel like doing step three today. Or they're in a hurry, so they skip step five and jump straight to the end. Or they're bored with the sequence, so they start mixing it up, doing step six before step two.

That's not a waltz anymore. That's someone flopping around on a dance floor looking like a fool.

The seven steps of a sale are the same. They exist in a specific sequence for specific reasons. Each one sets up the next. Skip one, and the whole thing gets cumbersome. Rearrange them, and you lose the customer before you ever get to the close.

This is something I want you to understand before we go through each step individually: the steps are not a menu. You don't get to pick and choose based on how you're feeling that day or how much time you think you have. You do them all, in order, every single time. That's what "consistency" actually means in practice.

Cars on Your Feet, Numbers on Your Seat

Before we go through the steps, there's one foundational rule of the process that you need to burn into your brain:

Cars on your feet, numbers on your seat.

It means this: the first three steps of the sale happen standing up. You're outside, you're moving, you're walking the lot, you're getting the customer into a car, and driving it. Those steps are active. The moment you sit down is the moment the process shifts from experience to negotiation, and that shift should happen with intention, not by accident.

Don't rush people to a desk before they've connected with a vehicle. Don't stand outside talking numbers when you should be walking inventory. Know which mode you're in, and stay in it until it's time to change.

The Seven Steps

Here is the full sequence. We'll spend a full chapter on each one, but I want you to see them together first so you understand how they connect.

Step 1: The Meet and Greet *Your first impression. Starts the moment they see you, not the moment you speak.*

Step 2: Set on a Vehicle in Stock *Qualifying the customer. Understanding their wants, their needs, and what they're really looking for.*

Step 3: Demo All Features The Test Drive *Walk around, demonstrate, and get them behind the wheel. This is where belief becomes experience.*

Step 4: Establish the Price. Sit down, present the numbers, and identify the *type of buyer you're working with.*

Step 5: Present to the Desk *Work with your manager to structure a deal. This is where strategy meets negotiation.*

Step 6: Close the Sale *Ask for the business. Handle objections. Guide the customer across the threshold.*

Step 7: Follow Up *The sale doesn't end when they drive off the lot. That's where the relationship begins.*

Seven steps. In that order. Every time.

Why the Order Matters

Let me give you a quick example of what happens when the sequence breaks down.

A new salesperson sees a customer walk onto the lot. They do a decent meet and greet, exchange names. So far, so good. Then, because they're nervous and trying to move things along, they immediately say: "So what kind of payment are you looking for?"

The customer hasn't driven anything. They haven't connected with a vehicle. They have no emotional investment in anything on that lot. And now you're asking them to commit to a payment number. What do you think happens?

They shut down. "We're just looking." Or they give you a completely unrealistic number, and now you've anchored the entire negotiation to a figure that doesn't work for anyone.

The payment question belongs in Step Four, not Step One. When you ask it in the right place, after the customer has driven a vehicle they actually like and have started to imagine themselves owning it, you get a completely different answer. Because now they're invested. Now they want the car. Now the number is a problem to solve together, not a reason to leave.

Sequence is not just a formality. It's a strategy.

FROM THE FLOOR

Early in my career, I thought I knew more than I did. Most new salespeople do. You learn the steps, you feel confident, and then a customer does something unexpected, and you improvise rather than sticking to the process.

A customer came onto the lot, found a car he liked, and we moved through the first three steps cleanly. Meet-and-greet, set up on a vehicle, walked around it, and demoed the features. Then I got to the test drive, and he waved me off. Said he didn't need to drive it; he'd seen enough, he was ready to talk numbers.

I was thrilled. We're moving fast. He likes the car. Let's go inside and write this up.

We sat down. I took his application. We went through the four-square, negotiated the numbers, and went back and forth with the desk. The whole process took close to two hours. We were working toward a deal.

And then, right at the end, he leaned back and said he never really got a chance to drive the vehicle. Said it to my manager. Said it like it was news.

I knew that wasn't accurate. But you can't call a customer a liar and expect to sell them a car. So I stood there.

Then came the part that hurt. He told me he wanted to bring his wife back, take a test drive, and see how she felt about it. And he left.

He never came back.

My sales manager was unhappy. The desk was unhappy. And I stood there knowing exactly what had happened. I had let a customer talk me out of Step Three. And without the test drive, he never got behind the wheel. Never felt the engine. Never smelled the interior. Never sat in the seat and thought: This is mine. I didn't give him any mental ownership of that vehicle, and when it came time to make a decision, he didn't have enough invested to make one.

Had I held the process, had I found a way to get him into the driver's seat even briefly, even just to pull it around the lot, even just to ask him to park it in his driveway and see if it fit the garage, the story ends differently. Instead, I let him direct the sale, and he walked.

That customer taught me something I never forgot: the test drive is not optional. It's not a formality you skip when the customer seems ready. It's the step where they stop thinking about the car and start feeling it. And feeling it is what closes deals.

A Word on Time

One of the things new salespeople often get wrong is thinking that following all 7 steps will take too long. They worry about losing the customer if they move too slowly.

Here's the truth: a rushed sale loses more customers than a thorough one. When customers feel pushed, they push back. When they feel guided, they follow.

The steps don't need to take forever. An experienced salesperson can move through them efficiently and still do every single one. But they can't be skipped. The customer needs each step to build confidence in you, in the vehicle, and in the decision they're about to make.

Give them what they need. The time is worth it.

"The Rule: The steps are the dance. Follow the sequence every time, and the sale flows. Skip a step, and you're flailing on the floor."

CHAPTER 5

THE FOUR TYPES OF BUYERS

THE MOST IMPORTANT THING Nobody Teaches You and Why It Changes Everything

Before we go through the seven steps in detail, there's something you need to understand that will change the way you approach every negotiation you ever have.

Not every customer cares about the same thing.

That sounds obvious when I say it out loud. But you'd be amazed at how many salespeople treat every customer as if they all have the same priority. They hammer on price with someone who doesn't care about price. They push payments on someone who's only thinking about their trade. They waste twenty minutes on the wrong number while the real issue sits right in front of them, completely ignored.

Here's the truth: there are exactly four types of buyers. Once you learn to identify which type you're dealing with, you stop working against the customer and start working with them. You stop talking about the things that don't matter to them and start focusing on the one thing that does.

This is one of the most valuable frameworks I can give you. Learn it. Use it every time.

The Four Types

Type 1: The Cash Buyer
Their focus: *the vehicle's price.*

The cash buyer may or may not have a trade. They may or may not care about monthly payments. None of that is what brought them in today. Their entire focus is on one thing: the car's price. That is it. They either want to know what you are asking, or they already have a number in their head, and they are not going over it. The difference between their trade and the vehicle price does not interest them. The monthly payment can be figured out later. Right now, they want to know if you can sell them this car at a price that works for them. Do not make the mistake of hammering payments on someone who has not once mentioned payments. Do not push the trade conversation if they have not brought it up. Read the room. If price is all they are talking about, then price is all you work with. Stay on what matters to them, and you will get to a deal a lot faster than the salesperson who keeps selling in the wrong direction.

Type 2: The Trade Allowance Buyer
Their focus: *How much you're giving them for their vehicle.*

This is the customer who is emotionally invested in their trade. Maybe they have had the car for years. Maybe it was passed down from a family member. Maybe they have taken immaculate care of it and have every service record since day one. Whatever the reason, they have a number in their head for what that car is worth, and that number matters to them more than almost anything else in the deal. Do not aggressively tear down their trade. That will put them on defense immediately, and you will lose the goodwill you worked hard to build. Instead, plant a few seeds. Walk around their vehicle naturally and let the conversation do the work. Something like: looks like you have taken good care of this car, those tires are getting a little worn though, when did you last replace them? Or you notice a small door ding and say, "Was that a grocery cart?" Now they are thinking about the tires they need to replace and the ding they stopped noticing years ago. Things that affect value without you ever having to say the word value. You are not attacking their car. You are gently reminding them that their car is not perfect, which they already know, but have stopped seeing. That subtle shift makes the trade conversation much easier when the numbers come out. Do not over-praise the trade either. Build expectations you cannot meet, and you will pay for it at the desk. Find out what they are expecting, acknowledge what is genuinely good about the vehicle, and work from there.

Type 3: The Difference Buyer

Their focus: *The gap between what they're trading and what they're buying.*

This customer has already done the math before they walked through the door. They know the car they are looking at. They know what they expect from their trade. And they have a very specific number in their head for what they are willing to pay out of pocket after the trade is applied. That number is not a suggestion. It is their line. They do not particularly care how you get there. Raise the trade, lower the price, restructure the deal, do whatever you need to do on your end. That is your problem to solve, not theirs. What they care about is that the difference between what they are buying and what they are trading comes out where they need it to be. If you spend twenty minutes working on payments with this buyer, you are wasting everyone's time. If you hammer on the price without addressing the trade, you will get nowhere. They are not listening to any of that. They are doing one calculation in their head and waiting for your answer to match it. Find a way to address their difference, and you have a deal. Miss it, and they will walk out just as calmly as they walked in, because they already knew their number before you said a word.

Type 4: The Payment Buyer

Their focus: *The monthly payment.*

This is by far the most common buyer you will encounter, and under-standing them is critical to your success on the floor. Most of your customers will be making payments. Whether they are financing through their own bank, their credit union, or your dealership's finance department, they came in with a number in mind. Not a price. Not a trade value. A monthly payment. That is the number they discussed with their spouse before leaving the house. That is the number they typed into a payment calculator on their phone last night. That is the number they are sitting across from you, thinking about right now.

You will often know you have a payment buyer before they ever sit down. Pay attention to what they are saying to each other on the lot before they even know you are listening. You overhear one spouse say to the other, "Do you think we can afford the payment on this one?" Or a customer walks up, and the first thing out of their mouth is: " How much are the payments on this"? That is your signal. They just told you exactly how to sell them without realizing it. File it away and use it.

They may not lead with it directly once the conversation starts. In fact, they might spend twenty minutes talking about price, trade, and everything in between. Do not be fooled. Acknowledge what they are saying, work the conversation, but always be steering toward the payment. That is where the deal lives for this buyer.

Here is something that works in your favor with payment buyers. Term length is your quiet lever. A longer term brings the payment down without touching the price or the trade. Use it when you need to, but do not bring it up with the customer unless you absolutely have to. The moment you start talking terms, you are putting a roadblock in front of yourself that you will have to climb over later. Let the finance office handle the term. Your job is to get the payment close enough that the customer says yes, and the desk has something real to work with.

This is also the easiest buyer type to work with once you understand them. A monthly payment is a much smaller number than a purchase price, and smaller numbers are easier to move. A customer who will not budge on a $30,000 price tag will often accept a payment that is fifteen dollars higher per month without blinking. Work on the payment. Stay out of your own way on term. And keep the conversation focused on getting them into the vehicle they want at a number they can live with every month.

Why This Matters More Than You Think

I'll give you a real example. A few years ago, my wife decided she wanted to buy a new car on her own. I supported the idea that every adult should experience the process at least once. I told her: Don't sign anything until I get there, but go ahead and start, and I will review the deal before you sign.

She went to a dealership looking to trade in her current vehicle. Before she ever walked through the door, I helped her establish what her trade was actually worth. We went online through Carvana, entered all the vehicle details, condition, mileage, trim level, and within minutes, we had an offer. Thirteen thousand dollars. Not an estimate. Not a rough ballpark. An actual written offer from a company that buys cars every day to resell them. That is as close to real market value as you are going to get from any source outside of selling it yourself.

Here is the lesson for you, as a salesperson. Customers are doing this before they walk onto your lot. They are going online, getting offers from Carvana, CarMax, and other instant-buy services, and walking in knowing exactly what their trade is worth in the current market. You need to know this going in. If a customer tells you they have an outside offer on their trade, get that number early in the conversation. And if you are advising a friend or family member who is going to trade in a vehicle, tell them what I told my wife. Get the offer in writing before you go to the dealership. Print it out or pull it up on your phone. A written offer from a legitimate buying service is one of the strongest negotiating tools a trade allowance buyer has, and a good salesperson will respect it rather than fight it.

The dealership inspected her car and offered $8,000. She showed them the Carvana offer. After some back-and-forth, they settled on $13,000. She's a trade allowance buyer. The trade was the issue. Once it was resolved, everything else could move.

But here's where it went wrong on the dealership's end. Even after the trade was settled, they spent the next two hours hammering her on payments. Payments, payments, payments. That's not what she came in for. She'd already told them how she wanted to handle financing. They weren't listening.

They never identified what type of buyer they had, so they spent two hours selling in the wrong direction.

By the time I arrived, she was frustrated. I walked in, sat down, and told the finance manager clearly: "We know our rate; here's what we'll accept, and the only add-on we're considering is gap insurance." We eventually added an extended warranty, but only after the finance manager sat down with us like a professional and presented it properly. Not at six thousand dollars. At nineteen hundred, which was reasonable for what it covered.

The whole ordeal took far longer than it needed to, and the reason was simple. Nobody on that sales floor was paying attention. My wife was telling them exactly what mattered to her from the moment she arrived. It was in her conversations. It was in her questions. It was what she kept coming back to every time the salesperson tried to redirect her. The trade. That was her issue, and she never stopped talking about it. But nobody was listening.

This is why the qualifying conversation matters so much before you ever get to numbers. When a customer walks onto your lot, they are already telling you how to sell them. You just have to be paying attention. Ask open-ended questions and then be quiet. Let them talk. What are you looking to do with your current vehicle? What are you hoping to get out of it? How long have you had it? Those are not just small talk questions. They are intelligence gathering. A customer who answers those questions is handing you a roadmap to their deal before you have shown them a single vehicle.

Had anyone on that floor asked the right questions early in the conversation, they would have known immediately that my wife was a trade allowance buyer. Everything else, the payments, the price, the financing, would have fallen into place once the trade was resolved. Instead, they spent two hours selling in the wrong direction because nobody stopped long enough to find out what actually mattered to the person sitting across from them.

How to Identify Which Type You Have

You find this out during Step Two, the qualifying conversation. It's not a formal survey. You're just paying attention to what the customer emphasizes.

Do they keep coming back to the vehicle's price? Cash buyer.

Are they talking about their trade? Describing it in detail, mentioning what they paid for it, what they've done to it, and what someone told them it's worth? Trade allowance buyer.

If the customer mentions early in the conversation what they hope to walk away paying after their trade is applied, or what they want their out-of-pocket number to be once everything is settled, you are most likely looking at a difference buyer. They did not wait for you to ask. They volunteered it because that number has been on their mind since before they arrived. Are they asking about payments before you've even talked about the car? Payment buyer.

Sometimes customers will tell you directly. More often, you'll pick it up from the pattern of what they keep returning to. Either way, the moment you know, your entire approach shifts. You stop working on the boxes that don't matter and pour your energy into the one that does.

One More Thing: Don't Ignore the Other Boxes

Knowing a customer's type does not mean you abandon the other three squares. It means you know which box to protect and which boxes give you room to work.

If your customer is a payment buyer, you have more flexibility on price and trade as long as the payment lands where it needs to be. Work those levers quietly and get the payment to a number they can live with. That is the close.

If your customer is a trade allowance buyer, the trade number is the line you have to get across. You may be able to give a little on the vehicle price to make the trade work, but do not deviate from the price unless there is absolutely no trade involved in the deal. The moment you start dropping the price on a trade allowance buyer without resolving the trade first, you have given away gross you did not need to give, and you still have not solved their actual problem. Resolve the trade first. Hold the price unless the deal requires otherwise.

The four types tell you where the customer's line is. Your job is to figure out how to get them across it without giving away more than you have to.

Know their type early, protect the right box, and work everything else to get the deal done.

FROM THE FLOOR

Early in my career, I had a customer who wanted to buy a car. He told me as much. He said, "Go find out if this is going to work." I'm not going to waste my time.

I froze. I didn't know how to ask for a deposit. I was afraid he'd say no. So I went to my manager and told him the customer wanted to move forward, but I didn't have a check.

My manager looked at me and said, "Go back and get a check. I'm not working this without something."

So I went back to the customer and tried to ask. I fumbled it. The customer stood up. He was done. He was walking out.

I turned the deal over to another salesperson. That salesperson sat down across from the customer, looked him in the eyes, and said: "I don't see any reason this isn't going to be a car deal. Let me need a check to hold this for you while I present it."

The customer wrote the check.

They sold the car. That salesperson got the commission. I got half because I'd done the legwork for half of what should have been entirely mine.

The lesson is simple: ask for the check. Ask directly and confidently, like it's the most natural thing in the world. Because in this business, it is.

"The Rule: Numbers on your seat, commitment on paper. Not every dealer-ship requires a deposit, but every deal requires a commitment. Get the initial. Ask for the deposit if required. Then go fight for them."

CHAPTER 6

STEP ONE: THE MEET AND GREET

THE SALE STARTS BEFORE You Say a Word

I want you to think about the last time you walked into a business to spend your own money.

Before anyone spoke to you. Before a single word was exchanged. You already had a feeling. You knew whether you felt welcome or whether you felt like you were interrupting someone's day. You knew whether the person who was going to help you looked like someone you wanted to deal with or someone you'd rather avoid. You made all of those judgments in about ten seconds, probably without even realizing it.

That's exactly what your customers are doing to you the moment they pull onto the lot.

This is why the meet-and-greet is the most important step in the entire sales process. Not because it's the most complicated, it's actually the simplest thing you'll do all day. But you can lose a customer here before the conversation ever begins. And most salespeople do, more often than they realize.

The Ten-Second Rule

Researchers who study first impressions generally agree that people form their initial judgment of a new person within seconds, sometimes as few as two or three. In a sales environment, call it ten seconds to be generous. In ten seconds, the customer has already decided several things about you.

Are you confident or uncertain?

Are you approachable or intimidating?

Do you look like someone who can help them, or someone who's going to be a problem?

You don't get a second chance at those ten seconds. They happen whether you're ready or not. The only question is whether you've decided what those ten seconds are going to communicate.

The salespeople who understand this show up intentionally. They've made choices about their appearance, their posture, their energy before they ever walk out the door. They don't leave their first impression to chance.

Neither should you.

It Starts the Moment They See You

Let me be precise about something: the meet-and-greet does not begin when you walk up and say hello. It begins the moment the customer sees you.

From inside their car, before they've even turned off the engine, they're already watching. They're watching how you carry yourself on the lot. They're watching whether you look alert or distracted. They're watching whether you're on your phone, leaning against a car looking bored, or in the middle of a conversation with a coworker that you clearly don't want to leave.

Customers observe more than most salespeople realize. And what they observe in those first few seconds before you've done anything, before you've said anything, is already shaping their decision about whether to get out of that car.

I've watched cars pull onto a lot, take a slow loop, and drive right back out. Not because the inventory was wrong. Not because the price was wrong. Because of what they saw when they looked at the people standing on that lot. That's a sale that was lost before it ever had a chance.

Before we talk about what to say, we need to discuss what you're already communicating.

What You're Communicating Before You Speak

Your appearance sends a message. It doesn't have to be expensive. It has to be appropriate and professional for your environment. A high-end luxury store calls for a different standard than a buy here, pay here lot, and dressing too formally for a BHPH environment can actually create distance between you and your customer. The goal is to mirror the environment you're in while still appearing to be someone who takes their job seriously.

Whatever the dress standard is at your dealership, meet it. Better yet, exceed it slightly. Clean clothes, clean shoes, groomed appearance. If it's raining, have a raincoat. If it's cold, dress for it. I've watched salespeople lose customers before they even reached them because they came outside completely unprepared for the weather. Your customer drove 30 minutes in the rain to get here. The least you can do is be ready to walk the lot with them.

Your posture sends a message. Standing upright, aware of your surroundings, with your head up, communicates confidence and readiness. Slouching against a car, hands in your pockets, eyes on your phone, communicates that helping someone is an inconvenience. Customers read this immediately and respond accordingly.

Your energy sends a message. This is the hardest one to fake, which is why I spent a full chapter on the Disneyland Principle before we got here. Customers can tell whether you're genuinely glad they showed up or just going through the motions. The ones who feel the difference will tell you with their feet. They'll walk.

The Acknowledgment

Here's where most salespeople make one of two mistakes: they either ignore the customer for too long, or they sprint toward them the moment they step out of the car like they've been waiting behind a starting gate.

Both are wrong. Both feel bad for the customer. And both communicate the same underlying message: this salesperson is either not paying attention or is desperate.

What works is the simple acknowledgment. The moment you see a customer arrive, you acknowledge them. Not by rushing over. Not by shouting from across the lot. A nod of the head. A small wave. A friendly "Hi folks, I'll be right with you" from a comfortable distance.

That small gesture does three things at once. It tells the customer they've been seen. It tells them help is available. And it gives them a moment to settle in without feeling ambushed. You've already exceeded their expectations, because what most of them came in braced for was exactly that ambush.

Then you walk over at a normal pace. Not rushing, not dragging your feet. With purpose, but without urgency. Hands visible. Head up the energy of someone comfortable in their environment and glad to help.

The Introduction

Keep it simple. This is not the moment for clever openers or practiced lines. Customers don't want a performance. They want a person.

Hi, my name is [your name]. Welcome to [dealership name]. How can I help you today?

That's it. Friendly, clear, professional. Notice what's not in there: "What are you here to buy?" or "What are you looking for today?" Those questions put the customer on defense before you've earned the right to ask them anything. You haven't built any trust yet. You haven't given them any reason to open up. You're just a stranger asking them to commit to something.

"How can I help you today?" is different. It's open. It's service-oriented. It positions you as someone who is there for them, not someone trying to extract something from them. The answer to that question tells you everything you need to know to begin, and the customer gave it to you voluntarily.

The Business Card Question

The general rule for business cards during the meet-and-greet is simple: hold off until you have earned it. At the moment of introduction, you are a stranger. You have not done anything for this customer yet. You have not earned their attention, their trust, or their contact information. Handing them a card at that stage is presumptuous at best, and at worst it reads as aggressive, as if you are trying to stake your claim before you have given them any reason to choose you.

You know what happens to most of those cards? I have picked hundreds of them up off the ground at dealerships. They go in a pocket and end up in the trash.

That said, there are situations where offering a card upfront makes sense. If you are the only salesperson on duty and there is no possibility of a mandatory turn, go ahead and card them early. If you work at a high-end store where turns just don't happen, same thing. If you know with complete certainty that this customer will be yours from start to finish, a card at the beginning does no harm.

But in most dealerships, mandatory turns are part of the culture. Another salesperson or manager may end up working with this customer before the deal is done. If you hand your card to a customer at the door and they get turned to someone else twenty minutes later, you have created an awkward situation for everyone and potentially a commission dispute on top of it.

The safer play in most situations is to wait. Give them your card after you have provided value. After you have listened to them, helped them find something, and done something that makes them want to remember who you are. That is when the card means something. That is when they will actually keep it.

Acknowledge Everyone

This is non-negotiable: if a customer comes in with other people, you greet every single one of them.

I cannot tell you how many deals I've watched die because a salesperson focused on the person who spoke first, ignoring everyone else. A husband and wife walk in, the husband starts talking, and the salesperson talks to the husband for twenty minutes while the wife stands there feeling invisible. And then every time the wife looks at the husband and says something like "I'm ready to go." And they leave. And the salesperson is standing there saying, "They were just looking."

They were not just looking. The wife was making a decision. And the decision she made was that she didn't feel respected, so that she wouldn't spend her family's money there.

Here's the truth about spouses: in most cases, the woman is the real decision maker. That's not a generalization, that's experience. The man might drive the conversation, but if she's not on board, the deal is dead. Happy wife, happy life is not just a saying. It's a closing strategy.

So when a couple walks in, and the husband introduces himself but doesn't introduce his wife, you turn to her and say: "And you are?" Simple. Respectful. It takes two seconds, and it tells her that she matters in this conversation.

If there are children, acknowledge them too. Say hello. Ask their names if they're old enough. Parents notice when someone treats their kids with respect, and it creates goodwill faster than almost anything else you can do.

Are You Here to See Anyone?

Always ask this before you go any further. It is one of the most important questions you will ever ask on the sales floor, and it costs you nothing to ask it early.

If a customer called the internet department last week, or stopped by three days ago and spoke to another salesperson, and you take the up without asking, you are going to spend thirty minutes with them before they mention it. At that point, you have to turn them over to whoever they originally spoke with. You just wasted half an hour and got nothing.

Ask it early. Have you been in before, or is this your first time visiting us? Clean, simple, no awkwardness. If they have a relationship with someone else at the store, find that person first before you do anything else.

Here is what not to do. Do not make excuses for the other salesperson. Do not tell the customer they are at lunch, with another customer, or out on a test drive. None of that is the customer's concern, and none of it helps you. What you do is find that salesperson immediately. If they are unavailable, let the customer know their salesperson will be right with them and offer to help them feel comfortable while they wait. If the salesperson is available, let them know their customer is here and either have them greet them or turn them over to you properly.

I learned this lesson the hard way. A customer came in and asked for John. John was at lunch. Instead of going to get John, I told the customer John was at lunch, but that I would be happy to help them. The customer said it was fine and did not want to disturb his lunch. So I took them. We walked the lot, found a vehicle they liked, did the test drive, worked the numbers, and sat down at the desk. We were close to a deal when John walked by. The customer lit up. Hey John, great to see you. We did not want to bother you at lunch, so this salesperson here has been taking great care of us. John smiled, said, "No problem at all, you guys have a great day," and kept walking.

After the sale, John came to find me. He was polite about it, but the message was clear. Thanks for selling my car for me, he said. But you did not get me, so that is my commission. He was right. I had taken his customer, worked the deal, closed the sale, and John collected 100% of the commission, finishing his lunch without missing a bite.

The rule is simple. If a customer comes in asking for someone who is in the building, get that person first. Always. No exceptions. If the salesperson is out for the day, that is a different story, and you can proceed. But if they are anywhere on the premises, check in with them before you do anything else. Let them know their customer is here. Let them decide whether to greet them, have you take them, or properly turn them over to you. That decision belongs to them, not to you.

Always ask. Always find out. It takes 30 seconds and protects your commission, your relationships with coworkers, and your reputation on the floor.

Three Stories That Show You Exactly What Not to Do
STORY ONE: THE FURNITURE STORE

I walked into a well-known furniture store looking for a recliner. Three salespeople were sitting on a showroom couch playing on their phones. I could hear them, in earshot, debating whose turn it was to help me like it was a burden. Like I was interrupting something important.

The one who drew the short straw walked over and said, without a greeting, without a smile, without even telling me his name: "What are you here to buy today?"

My answer was immediate. "Nothing. I'm just looking. I'll let you know if I need help."

And I meant it. They'd lost me in the first five seconds. I didn't buy a thing. Went somewhere else.

STORY TWO: THE TEXAS HEAT

My wife and I pulled onto a dealership lot on a hot afternoon, ninety-five degrees, which is nothing unusual in Texas. We got out and started walking the inventory. Three salespeople were standing on an elevated deck watching us from a distance.

Nobody moved.

They just stood there and watched while we walked around their lot looking at vehicles. I am not going to walk up to a platform and beg someone to help me spend money. So we got back in the car and drove to the dealership next door. Bought a car there the same afternoon.

STORY THREE: THE SPRINT

I was sitting in the front lobby of a dealership I managed with a glass-front wall and a full view of the lot. A car pulled in. Two salespeople inside the showroom both saw it at the same time. They jumped up, ran for the door, and literally shoved each other, trying to get through it first, pushing and shoving like it was a race.

The customers, still in their car, watched every second of this.

The one who won was out of breath when he got there. He stuck his hand out and started shaking the man's hand before he'd even introduced himself, and never looked at the wife. Never acknowledged the kids in the back seat. Just started talking.

The family looked around for a few minutes and left.

When I asked what happened, the salesperson said: "They were just looking."

No. They were watching. And what they saw told them everything they needed to know.

The Meet and Greet Checklist

Before we move on, here is a simple checklist. Run through it mentally every time a customer arrives.

✓ Appearance is appropriate and professional for the environment

✓ Phone is in your pocket, not in your hand

✓ You acknowledged the customer before approaching, nod, wave, or a brief greeting from a distance

✓ You approached at a normal walking pace, not running

✓ You introduced yourself by name

✓ You asked how you can help them, not what they're here to buy

✓ You greeted every person in the group, including children

✓ You asked whether they're here to see anyone

✓ You did not hand them a business card

✓ You did not ask about payment, trade, or budget yet

Ten items. None of them is complicated. All of them are trainable. The salespeople who do all ten, every time, consistently outperform the ones who do seven or eight and think that's close enough.

Close enough is not the standard. Every time is the standard.

FROM THE FLOOR

One afternoon, I was at my desk when I noticed a customer pull into the lot in a taxi, which caught my attention immediately. Most customers drive themselves. This one stepped out of the cab and walked directly toward a specific vehicle, as if he knew exactly what he was looking for. No wandering. No browsing. He had a destination in mind before he ever got out of the car.

I did not rush. I stood up, walked out at a normal pace, and gave him a small wave as I approached. When I reached him, I introduced myself and said I would be happy to help if he had any questions.

He told me he had just gotten off a flight and came straight from the airport. His vehicle had been destroyed in a fire in the airport parking lot while he was traveling. He had seen one of our ads and came directly to us. He knew which vehicle he wanted. He just needed to drive it and confirm it.

We took a short test drive. Came back. He asked how to make out the check.

Now, here is where many salespeople make a critical mistake. The deal was done. The customer had made his decision before he ever stepped out of that taxi. But I have watched salespeople in situations exactly like this one keep talking. Keep selling. Keep throwing features and benefits at a customer who already bought the car in their head twenty minutes ago. They talk themselves right out of a deal that was already closed.

When the customer is ready, stop selling. Follow their lead. The taxi customer did not need me to explain the warranty options, walk him through the financing packages, or tell him about the extended service plan. He needed a pen and a place to write a check. That was it. My job in that moment was to get out of the way and let him buy the car.

Know when to sell and know when to stop. The best salespeople in this business understand that listening is a skill just as important as talking. When a customer commits, verbally or through their actions, your job shifts immediately. You are no longer selling. You are facilitating. There is a significant difference, and learning to recognize that moment is what separates salespeople who occasionally get lucky from salespeople who consistently close.

Start to finish, that deal took maybe 45 minutes. It was easy because the approach was right. No pressure, no assumptions, no rushing, and most importantly, no overselling once the customer showed me he was ready. Just a professional greeting, a short test drive, and a willingness to follow his lead all the way to the close.

Not every customer comes in ready to buy. But every customer deserves that same professional approach. And every salesperson needs to know when to put the pitch down and pick up the pen.

You never know which one will be the taxi customer.

"The Rule: The meet and greet starts the moment they see you. From that instant, you are either building trust or destroying it. Make sure you're doing it on purpose."

CHAPTER 7

STEP TWO: SET ON A VEHICLE IN STOCK

FINDING OUT WHAT THEY Really Want and What They May Actually Need

Here's something most new salespeople get wrong from the very beginning.

They hear what the customer says they want, and they find it. The customer says they want a red truck, and the salesperson goes out looking for one. The customer says they want a small sedan, and the salesperson shows them small sedans. Simple, right?

Except it's not that simple. Because what a customer says they want and what they may actually need at times are often two completely different things. And your job, if you're doing it right, is to understand both, and then help them find something that satisfies both of them, if possible.

That's what Step Two is really about, not just finding a vehicle, but understanding the client.

Walk Your Inventory Every Morning

Before we talk about how to have the qualifying conversation, let's talk about something you should be doing before your first customer of the day ever arrives.

Walk your inventory.

Every morning, before you take an up, you should know where every vehicle on your lot is, what equipment it has, and what makes it different from the one next to it. This sounds basic. Most salespeople don't do it consistently. And the ones who don't pay for it every time a customer asks for something specific.

There's another reason this matters: inventory changes constantly. Vehicles get sold, traded, moved to detail, relocated for display, parked in service, or transferred from another store. What was sitting on the front line yesterday may be gone this morning. A vehicle that just arrived may be exactly what your next customer wants, and if you haven't walked the lot, you won't even know it exists.

It doesn't take long. On a normal-sized lot, you can walk your inventory in just a few minutes every morning. If your dealership has six acres of vehicles and supplies golf carts, then take a golf cart ride every day. The point is simple: look at your inventory daily.

Picture this: a customer comes in looking for a half-ton truck with a V6 diesel and a tow package. You nod confidently and say, "I think we might have something like that," and then spend the next ten minutes wandering around the lot squinting at window stickers while the customer watches. That's not a professional. That's someone who wasn't prepared.

Now picture the salesperson who smiles and says: I think I have exactly what you are looking for, follow me. No long explanation. No rattling off specs in the parking lot. Just a confident invitation to walk with them. That person looks like they know where they are going. That person builds confidence before they have even touched a vehicle. The customer is already following them across the lot, thinking this person knows what they have out here. And that feeling, that quiet confidence in the person leading them, is worth more than any feature you could recite from a window sticker. Walk your inventory. Know your product. It costs you nothing but a few minutes every morning, and it pays off every single day.

Wants vs. Needs

Let me give you a simple example.

A man walks onto your lot and tells you he wants a half-ton pickup truck. That is his want. But before you start walking him toward the inventory, take a few minutes and have a casual conversation. Not an interrogation. Just a friendly back-and-forth that helps you understand what this truck actually needs to do for him.

Something like: "So, what are you planning to haul with it?" Got a boat? Camper? Just curious because I want to make sure we find you the right one. Most people do not realize how much towing capacity varies from truck to truck, and I would rather ask a few dumb questions now than put you in the wrong vehicle later.

If he mentions a boat or trailer, casually ask if he happens to know roughly how much it weighs when loaded. He may not know exactly, and that is fine. But if he says something like, " Oh, it is probably around ten or twelve thousand pounds, you now know a half ton is not going to cut it, and you have that information without ever making him feel like he walked into a technical seminar.

Also worth asking is whether the boat or trailer he mentioned is the main thing he plans to tow, or if he also pulls anything else from time to time. People forget to mention the fifth wheel camper they borrow twice a year or the utility trailer they use for landscaping. A truck is a long-term purchase, and a couple of casual questions now can save both of you a significant headache down the road.

Then fill in the rest of the picture. Family of five means cab space matters. Forty miles of highway every day means fuel economy matters. Maybe the half ton works perfectly once you know everything. Maybe the conversation leads him to realize he actually needs a three-quarter ton. Either way, you cannot make the right call until you understand the full situation. And the full situation comes out naturally when you ask the right questions in the right way.

You are the professional in this conversation. The customer knows what he wants. Your job is to make sure what he wants is actually what he needs. A few casual questions at the beginning save everyone a lot of trouble later.

How to Ask the Right Questions

The qualifying conversation isn't an interrogation. It's a conversation with a purpose. You're trying to understand the customer's situation well enough to guide them to the right vehicle, and you're doing it in a way that feels natural rather than procedural.

Start broad and get specific. "What are you looking to use this vehicle for?" is a great opening because it invites them to tell you their story. From there, you follow what they give you.

If they mention family, ask about family. How many kids? How old? Do they need car seats? Do they need room for a stroller? Are they doing sports travel, weekend trips, or school runs?

If they mention work, ask about work. Is this their personal vehicle, or does it double as a work vehicle? Do they need to haul equipment? Drive clients? Cover long distances?

If they mention towing, you need to be precise. Know your vehicles' tow ratings before making any representations. If you tell a customer a vehicle can handle a load it can't, you could be held liable when something goes wrong on the road. Get it right.

The goal of these questions is twofold. First, you're gathering the information you need to show them the right vehicle. Second, and just as importantly, you're building a connection. When you ask someone about their family, their work, and their weekend plans, and you actually listen to the answers, you stop being a salesperson and start being someone they're talking to. That relationship is what makes everything else easier.

Responding vs Answering

There is a difference between a response and an answer, and understanding that difference will save you more deals than almost anything else in this book.

An answer is exact and final. A response acknowledges the question and moves the conversation forward without locking you into something you cannot deliver yet.

Here is a simple example. A customer asks what time it is. An answer is 11:52 AM. A response is about noon. Same information, different level of commitment. In everyday life, it does not matter much. In car sales, it matters enormously.

When a customer asks how much the car is, before you have had any qualifying conversation, you do not have enough information to give them an accurate number. You do not know their trade situation, credit, down payment, or the terms they are working with. An answer at that stage is either a guess or a number that will come back to haunt you later.

A response sounds like this: " That depends on a few things we still need to go over together, but my job is to make sure we find a number that works for you.

When they ask what you will give them for their trade, our appraisal team determines that based on condition, mileage, and current market value, and I want to make sure you get every dollar it is worth. Let me get that process started for you.

You have acknowledged the question. You have given them something useful. And you have not painted yourself into a corner with a number you may not be able to deliver.

Only answer when you have enough information to answer accurately. Until then, respond and keep moving forward.

What "I'm Just Looking" Actually Means

Every salesperson who has spent more than a week on the floor has heard this phrase. And every new salesperson hears it as rejection.

It is not rejection. In my experience, it seldom is.

"I'm just looking" is a protective response. It is what people say when they are not ready to be pressured, when they are still getting comfortable with the environment, when something about the first interaction puts them slightly on guard. It means there is a wall up. Your job is to figure out what built it and take it down.

The right response is simple and pressure-free. That is perfectly fine. Take your time. I will be nearby if you see something you want to take a closer look at.

Then give them a moment. Do not follow them around. Do not hover. Let them breathe. More often than you would think, they will come back to you within a few minutes with a question. That question is your opening. The wall came down on its own because you did not push it.

There are more ways to handle this response than that one, and the right comeback depends on the customer, the situation, and what you are picking up from their energy. The bonus material available to readers of this book includes a full collection of I'm just looking responses you can study, practice, and make your own. You will find the link at the back of the book.

Sometimes the issue is not the customer at all. It is the salesperson. I once took a turn from a colleague who was getting nowhere with a woman at the used-car lot. He pulled me aside and told me she was just looking, that something was off, that he could not figure her out.

I walked over, introduced myself, and asked how I could help her.

She looked at me and said, "Thank God you are here." I really want to buy this car. But that other guy looks exactly like my ex-husband, and I cannot stand to look at him.

Nothing to do with the car. Nothing to do with the price. Nothing to do with the dealership. We test-drove the vehicle, negotiated fair numbers, and she drove home happy. The whole process took about ninety minutes once the right person was standing in front of her.

Do not take it personally. I'm just looking. Do not take it as a verdict. Take it as information. Something needs to change. Figure out what that something is and change it. Sometimes it is your approach. Sometimes it is your energy. And sometimes, as I learned that afternoon, it is simply you.

Don't Make Assumptions

Do not assume someone cannot afford new because they mentioned used. I have sold brand-new vehicles to customers who came in specifically asking about used cars because, once they saw what was available and understood the financing, new made more sense for them. The opposite is true, too. Someone who says they want new might be completely open to a certified pre-owned if it saves them several thousand dollars and still gives them what they need.

Do not assume that what a customer tells you they want is the final word on what they will actually buy. A customer walks in saying they want a red Cadillac Escalade. You walk your lot every morning, so you know exactly what you have, and you do not have a red Cadillac Escalade. You have two choices. Tell them you do not have one and watch them leave. Or say, "Follow me and show them what you do have." I cannot tell you how many times a customer walked off my lot because I did not have exactly what they asked for, and when I followed up later, I found out they had bought something completely different somewhere else. Not the red Escalade. Something else entirely caught their eye once they started looking. People come in with an idea. Ideas change when they see something that surprises them. Following me is always a better answer than saying, "I do not have that."

Do not assume the person speaking the most is the decision-maker. The quiet one is often the one making the call. Stay engaged with everyone in the group—every single one of them.

Do not assume you know what is important to them without asking. What matters to you about a vehicle might mean nothing to this customer, and what matters to them might be something you would never think to mention. Ask. Listen. Then respond to what they actually told you, not to what you thought they would say.

And do not assume that because you do not have exactly what they asked for, the deal is dead before it starts. Show them what you have. You might be surprised how often the car they end up buying isn't the one they came in looking for.

If You Don't Have Exactly What They Want

Here's a reality of the business: you won't always have the exact vehicle the customer describes. Wrong color, missing a feature, higher mileage than they wanted, whatever it is. This happens constantly. Your job is to bridge that gap without losing the momentum you've built.

The answer is to set on the closest thing you have. Find a vehicle that hits as many of their criteria as possible, acknowledge what's different, and get them into it anyway. Why? Because a customer who is sitting inside a vehicle, touching the controls, feeling the seat, that customer is a hundred times more likely to buy something than a customer who is standing in the lot looking at a list of inventory you might be able to locate.

If you do not have exactly what the customer is looking for, do not give up. Get with your manager. Many dealerships, including used-car lots with multiple locations, can search other stores in their network to locate a vehicle that meets the customer's needs. In some cases, they can even place an order. That is your manager's tool, not yours, so do not try to navigate that conversation alone. Bring them in and let them work that angle while you keep the customer engaged.

But even when a locate or an order is on the table, you still want to get the customer into something today. Find the closest thing you have on your lot and get them in it. The experience of sitting in a vehicle, feeling the seat, touching the controls, driving it down the road, is what converts interest into desire. A customer who has been behind the wheel of something close to what they want is emotionally invested in making a deal happen. Do not skip that step just because the exact spec is not sitting on your lot right now.

Mandatory Turns: Knowing When to Call for Help

Most dealerships have what's called a mandatory turn policy. If you've taken a customer through the process and you can't get them to commit, you're required to turn them over to another salesperson or a manager. This isn't a punishment. It's a system, and it exists for a good reason.

Sometimes the issue isn't the deal at all. Sometimes it's the personalities involved. The customer might have connected well with you up to a point, but now needs a different energy to get them across the line. Or they might need to hear the same thing from a different voice before they believe it. Or, as I've seen more than once, they might simply remind them of someone they don't like, and there's nothing you can do about that.

In my dealerships, we had a signal for turns. We all wore suits and ties. If a salesperson was adjusting their tie while out with a customer, that was the signal: come over, I need help. Another salesperson would naturally drift over, and the turn would happen without being obvious.

"Hey, glad I caught you. I have another appointment coming in, but this is [name], and I'd love for you to help them get into this vehicle."

Clean. Professional. No awkwardness for the customer. And the new salesperson starts fresh, without assumptions, from the beginning.

This is important: when you take a turn from another salesperson, start over. Don't inherit their version of the customer. Don't assume you know what the issue is based on a thirty-second hallway summary. Introduce yourself, ask how you can help, and let the customer tell you their story. You might find out something completely different from what you were told.

FROM THE FLOOR

The very first vehicle I leased was a Dodge Viper sold to a man in dirty work clothes who turned out to own a nine-story manufacturing plant. You'll read that story in Chapter Eighteen. The lesson here is the same one: never prejudge a customer based on what they look like.

"The Rule: Ask more than you talk. The customer will tell you exactly how to sell them if you're willing to listen."

CHAPTER 8

STEP THREE: DEMO ALL FEATURES AND THE TEST DRIVE

WHERE BELIEF BECOMES EXPERIENCE

Up to this point, everything has been conversation.

You've greeted the customer, built some comfort, asked the right questions, and found a vehicle that fits what they're looking for. You've done good work. But the customer is still in their head. They're still evaluating. They're still deciding whether this is the right choice.

Step Three is where that changes. This is where the vehicle stops being a concept and starts being an experience. And experience is what moves people from interested to committed.

The Walkaround

Before the test drive comes the walkaround. This is your chance to show the customer the vehicle in a way that directly connects with what they told you in Step Two. And that last part matters. You are not going through every item on the window sticker the same way for every customer. You are focusing on what they said was important to them and building your walkaround around that.

Start at the front of the vehicle: safety features, sensors, and lighting. Move around the exterior—body lines, fit, and finish. Open the hood if it makes sense for this customer. Then move into the cabin. Comfort, technology, power features, cargo space. Touch on everything, but slow down on what matters most to them.

If safety were their priority, maybe they mentioned an accident, maybe they are buying for a teenager, maybe they brought up a family member who got hurt, slow down on every safety feature. Show them how the automatic braking works. Walk them through the blind spot monitoring. Make it real and personal. And even if safety was not their main focus, bring it up anyway. Many buyers, especially women, appreciate knowing the vehicle they are getting into has been built with their safety in mind. You do not have to spend a lot of time on it, but mentioning it shows you care about more than just making a sale.

If they mentioned a long commute and fuel costs, talk about real-world fuel economy, the comfort of the driver's seat on an hour-long highway drive, and the features that make long drives less exhausting.

If they are buying for their family, open every door. Show them the legroom in the back. Let the kids climb in if they are there. Put something in the cargo area so they can picture it being used.

Keep it conversational. Keep it focused on them. You are not giving a presentation. You are having a conversation about their life and how this vehicle fits into it.

You are not showing them a car. You are showing them their life, improved.

Involve Them

A walkaround where you do all the talking and the customer does all the listening is a lecture. Lectures don't sell cars.

Open the door and invite them to sit in the driver's seat. Let them adjust it. Let them put their hands on the wheel. Let them reach for the controls and figure out where things are. Let them feel the seat and decide if it's comfortable. Ask them: "How does this fit?" "Do you have enough headroom?" "Is this the kind of display you're comfortable with?"

When they start touching things and asking questions, that's not an inconvenience; that's ownership beginning. The more they interact with the vehicle, the more it starts to feel like theirs. That feeling is enormously powerful in the decision-making process.

Pay attention to what they linger on. If a customer spends extra time on the sound system, ask them about it. If they keep looking at the cargo area, ask what they're planning to carry. If they smile when they adjust the seat, and it fits them perfectly, acknowledge it. "That's one of the things people love about this one."

Let them sell themselves. Your job is to guide the experience, not to fill every moment with talking.

Leading Them to the Test Drive

Here is one of the most important things I can teach you about this entire process, and I want you to write it down somewhere:

Never ask a customer if they want to test drive the car.

Never. Not once. Remove that question from your vocabulary entirely.

Here's why. When you ask someone if they want to do something, you're giving them the option to say no. And their default answer, especially for something that feels like a commitment, is almost always no. "Do you want to test drive it?" "No, I'm fine, I don't need to." And now you're stuck, because you've asked and they've answered, and pushing further feels like pressure.

Instead, you lead them into it.

I use the nursing home analogy in my training sessions: if you're caring for an elderly parent and you ask them, "Do you want to take a bath?" the answer is almost always no. But if you say, "All right, let's go get your bath," they get up and go. You're guiding them toward something you both know needs to happen. They always have the right to say no, but when you lead rather than ask, they most often follow.

So instead of asking, you just do it. "Let me grab the keys," and you go get the keys. When you come back, you say: "Why don't we hop in? I'll drive first so you can get a feel for the ride, then we'll switch."

Natural. Confident. No question mark at the end.

You Drive First

Always drive the vehicle off the lot. Always.

The customer is not familiar with this vehicle. They don't know how it responds, where the mirrors are, or how tight the turning radius feels. Asking them to navigate off a busy lot in an unfamiliar car while they're already slightly anxious is setting them up for a tense experience.

You take the wheel. You pull out, get to a safe area, a quiet street, a parking lot, wherever makes sense for your route, and then you switch. "Why don't you slide over and see how this feels for you?"

By the time they're in the driver's seat, the car is already moving. It's warmed up. The A/C is running. The seat is adjusted to something close to where they'll want it. The whole experience starts more comfortably.

Your Test Drive Route

Every salesperson needs a planned test drive route, and every manager needs to know what it is.

Why? Because things happen on test drives. Vehicles break down. Customers get distracted and end up going the wrong way. In the days before cell phones, this was a serious concern if the car didn't come back; someone needed to know where to look. Today, you have a cell phone, but the principle still applies: plan your route, know your route, communicate your route.

And build your route around right-hand turns.

I've said this in training for years: plan routes with as many right-hand turns as possible. Left turns mean crossing traffic. Crossing traffic is where accidents happen. You're in a vehicle the customer isn't familiar with, possibly in an area they don't know well, and they're slightly distracted because they're thinking about the car. Right turns keep it safer. It's a simple rule that most dealerships don't enforce, and it matters.

If the customer wants to deviate from the normal route, they want to see how it fits in their driveway, they want to take it on the highway, or they want to drive it past their mechanic, let your manager or a colleague know before you go. Just a quick heads-up. This isn't bureaucracy. It's common sense.

What to Do During the Drive

Here's the most common mistake salespeople make on a test drive: they talk the entire time.

They're narrating. They're explaining features. They're pointing at things. They're filling every moment of silence because they're nervous, and silence feels like failure.

Stop. Let the customer drive.

The test drive is not another sales presentation. The test drive is the moment the customer experiences the vehicle for themselves. Your voice interrupts that experience. Use it sparingly and intentionally.

Ask a few simple, well-timed questions. "How does this feel compared to what you're driving now?" "Do you notice the road noise?" "Is the visibility what you need?" These aren't interrogation questions; they're invitations for the customer to pay attention to specific things and articulate what they're feeling. Their answers move them closer to a decision without you having to push.

If they make a positive comment, they will acknowledge it. "That's one of the things people really love about this one." You're reflecting their positive experience to them. You're reinforcing without overselling.

And then be quiet again. Let them drive.

Paint a Picture of Ownership

While you have them in the car, you have an opportunity that you will not have anywhere else in the process. You can help them imagine what it would be like to own this vehicle.

Not in a manipulative way. In a genuine conversational way that connects the vehicle to what they told you about their life.

If they mentioned a long commute, with the adaptive cruise control, this seat, and the lane-keeping assist, your drive in is going to feel completely different. A lot of these newer vehicles will practically steer themselves on the highway. That is not a gimmick. After an hour on the road, you will feel the difference.

If they mentioned family road trips, imagine the kids in the back on a long drive. They have their own screen, rear climate control, and, actually, enough room to stretch out. Some of these vehicles now have built-in Wi-Fi hotspots so the kids stay connected and you stay sane.

While you are at it, point out some of the technologies that make daily driving easier and safer. Blind spot monitoring that alerts you when someone is in your blind spot. Automatic emergency braking that reacts faster than you can. A backup camera with cross traffic alert, so pulling out of a parking lot is no longer a guessing game. A heads-up display that puts your speed and navigation right on the windshield, so your eyes never leave the road. Wireless phone charging so they never have to dig for a cable. These features are common on many vehicles today, and most buyers do not even know to ask about them. Pointing them out during the drive creates value they did not know they were getting.

If they want to park it in a garage and are not sure it will fit, take it to their house. Seriously. If they live close by, drive over and park it in their driveway. I have done this more times than I can count, and it closes deals. Once a vehicle is parked in someone's driveway, and the neighbor comes out and says, "Wow, that looks great," the customer is already there mentally. You just need to get them to sign.

After the Drive

When you return to the dealership, don't pull the car back into the line. Pull it somewhere separate. Close to the door, visible, set apart from everything else on the lot. You want it isolated, this vehicle, their vehicle, not just one of fifty options they're still deciding between.

And when you get out, don't ask "What do you think?" That's too vague. It invites a noncommittal answer.

Ask something specific: "How does that compare to what you've been driving?" or "Could you see yourself in this every day?"

You're not asking them to buy it. You're asking them to imagine owning it. There's a difference, and it's an important one. The decision to buy comes from the imagination of ownership. Get them there first.

FROM THE FLOOR

I was on a test drive with two women who were partners, looking at a Chrysler convertible on a beautiful day in the Pacific Northwest. Eighty degrees, no wind, top was down. I was sitting in the back seat, demonstrating the vehicle as one of them drove. They were excited about the car. I was feeling confident about where the deal was headed.

Then a bird flew over and used my head as a target. Direct hit. Running down my face.

Both women completely lost it. I mean tears running down their faces, can't catch their breath laughing. I lost all credibility in that moment. Not because of anything I did wrong. Because of a bird.

I turned the deal over to another salesperson so I could get cleaned up. They ended up buying the car. They could not look me in the face for the rest of the process without dissolving into laughter again.

There is no lesson here except this: things happen. Some of them are completely outside your control. All you can do is handle it with grace, get out of the way when you need to, and add it to the collection of stories you'll be telling for the rest of your career.

FROM THE FLOOR

In thirty-five years, I have seen things happen on test drives that you could not script if you tried.

I once had a customer who wanted to take a vehicle out to see if it would fit in his driveway. Reasonable request. We have all done it. Sometimes I would even suggest it myself because getting a vehicle parked in someone's driveway is one of the best closing tools there is. Maybe a neighbor comes out and says it looks great, and suddenly the customer is already sold. So we headed out, no concerns, just a normal test drive with a logical destination.

We were sitting at a red light on the way to his house. Everything was fine—normal conversation. Then, without a word, he shifted the vehicle into park right there at the light, turned to me, and said, "I have to be honest with you." I do not actually need to see if it fits in the driveway. I just needed a ride home. Thank you very much. And he got out and walked away.

He had walked onto the lot on foot—no vehicle of his own. Just needed to get across town and figured a test drive was as efficient a method as any. I sat there at that green light for a moment, trying to process what had just happened before the car behind me reminded me to move.

Do not get angry. Do not take it personally. Drive back to the lot, walk into the break room, and tell the story. You just earned your place in the collection of things that only happen in this business.

Things happen on test drives. Stay professional, stay calm, and remember that every strange moment is just another story for the book.

"The Rule: Never ask if they want to test drive the car. Lead them to it. The experience of being in the vehicle is what converts interest into a decision."

CHAPTER 9

STEP FOUR: ESTABLISHING THE PRICE

*T*HE FOUR SQUARE, THE *Numbers, and the Art of Getting a Commitment*

This is where we sit down.

You've done the meet and greet. You've qualified the customer and found the right vehicle. You've walked around it, demonstrated its features, and taken a test drive. Now you come back to the dealership, and the process shifts cars on your feet, numbers on your seat. The active phase is done. Now it's time to talk business.

Most new salespeople dread this part. And honestly, the dread makes sense. This is where money gets discussed, where negotiations happen, where objections arise, and where deals fall apart. But here's something I want you to understand before we go any further: Step Four is not where deals die. Step Four is where deals get made. The difference between the two is almost always execution.

Do this well, and you'll close more than you think. Do it poorly, and you'll lose deals you should have won. Let's make sure you do it well.

Set the Stage

Before you sit down with numbers, do the basics. Bring the customer inside. Offer coffee and water, point out the restrooms, and whatever else your dealership provides. Get them comfortable. These are not just niceties.

They are tools. A customer who feels welcomed and settled is more open to conversation than one who feels rushed to a desk before they have caught their breath.

Make sure everyone who needs to be at the table is there. If a couple came in together, both of them sit down. If an adult child came to help a parent make a decision, they sit down too. You do not want to go back and forth presenting numbers to one person who then has to relay them to someone else. That kills momentum every single time. Get all the decision makers in the same room before you start.

Before you sit down, get yourself organized. Depending on your dealership, this might mean grabbing your tablet or iPad to open the app. Some stores do everything on a screen now. Others still use paper packets with the application, the worksheet, and the trade appraisal sheet. Know what your store uses and have it ready before you bring the customer inside.

Suppose there is a trade involved. Connect with your desk before you sit down with the customer. Give them the basic information on the trade. Year, make, model, mileage, and a quick condition assessment from your walkaround. They will give you a starter figure to work from when you get to the trade section of the four square. That number is not the final offer. It is your starting point. But having it before you sit down means you are not scrambling for information in front of the customer when the trade conversation starts.

Also, get the VIN off the trade before you go inside. Note the mileage. Do a quick walk around and note the condition. Ding on the passenger door, worn tires, cracked windshield, whatever you see. This takes three minutes, and it gives the desk what they need to give you something real to work with.

Being prepared when you sit down is part of being professional. Fumbling for paperwork, leaving the customer sitting while you find things, not knowing basic information about their trade, all of that communicates disorganization. And disorganization costs you trust at exactly the moment when trust matters most.

The Four Square

The four-square is a negotiation worksheet divided into four boxes. It has been the standard in dealerships for decades, and it is not going anywhere. The format may look different depending on where you work. Some stores still do it by hand on paper. Others generate it through their computer system and print it out for the customer. Some use a tablet and show it on screen. The tool itself may change, but the four boxes and what goes in them never do. Whether you are writing numbers by hand at a desk or handing a customer a printed sheet from your system, you are working the same four-square principle that salespeople have used for generations. Learn it cold. Understand what each box means and why it is there. The format your dealership uses is just the delivery method. The principle is what closes deals. The four boxes are:

Box 1: The Price of the Vehicle

This is where you start. Write in the retail price of the vehicle, and if there's an ADP sticker (Additional Dealer Profit, sometimes called a market adjustment), start there. The ADP exists because the dealership needs a negotiating cushion above MSRP. You'll negotiate down from it, aiming to land at or near MSRP without giving everything away in the first move. If the vehicle is on sale or has a current incentive, note it: "Retail price is $34,995, but it's currently on sale for $32,500, that's already $2,495 in savings." Reinforce the positives whenever you can.

Box 2: The Trade Allowance

If the customer has a trade, this is where it goes. Before you sit down, you've already gotten a starter figure from the desk manager, which they call the "hit figure." This is not the final number. It's the opening. The technique here is to deliver it in a way that gives you room to move without sounding like you're making it up. The line I used for years: "Last time we took in a vehicle similar to yours, I think they went somewhere around the area of [figure]. Is that what you were thinking?" That phrasing gives you four outs. You think. You believe. It was similar. It was somewhere around. You're not making a firm statement, you're probing. And you're finding out right now whether the customer is going to be reasonable or whether this trade is going to be the fight.

Box 3: The Down Payment

Banks love to see a third down on a fifteen-thousand-dollar vehicle that is five thousand dollars. Most customers do not have it, and that is fine. The number you write in this box is not a demand. It is an anchor.

Here is how to deliver it. Write the number down, slide the four-square across to the customer, point to the down payment box, and say something like: "Banks love to see about a third down on a vehicle like this, so we are going to start here at 5,000." Then put your pen down and stop talking.

Do not say another word.

This is one of the most important moments in the entire negotiation, and most new salespeople blow it by filling the silence. The first person who speaks after delivering that number loses. If you keep talking, you have taken the pressure off the customer to respond and signaled that you are not confident in the number you just put down. Let it sit. Let them process it. Let them be the ones to move.

When a customer sees five thousand dollars in the down payment box, a thousand dollars suddenly feels reasonable, even if they came in planning to put nothing down. You are moving them before the negotiation has even started. But only if you stay quiet long enough to let the anchor do its job.

Box 4: The Monthly Payment

This is the most important box for most customers, since they are payment buyers. They think in a monthly budget, not the total purchase price. Use this to your advantage. Come in high on the payment with the same kind of framing you used on the trade. "Last time I sold a vehicle like this, the customer was doing short-term financing, and the payment was around $850. I think there are longer-term options that could bring that down. What kind of payment were you thinking you could manage?" You're anchoring high, giving yourself a built-in out (short-term financing), and inviting them to give you a number. That number tells you everything you need to know about what you're working with.

Getting the Commitment

This is probably the most important moment in the entire process before you ever walk to the desk. Everything you have done up to this point has been building toward this. The customer is excited. They are mentally and verbally committing to buying a vehicle. Now you need to capture that commitment in a way that makes it real.

Once you have gone through all four boxes, circle the numbers that the customer has indicated they can work with. The vehicle price they're considering. The trade figure they are expecting. They can manage the down payment—the payment they can handle.

Then write a simple statement across the worksheet: I will purchase the above vehicle for the above terms.

Push it across the table, hand them a pen, and ask them to initial it.

This is not a contract. It is not legally binding. But here is what it is. It is the first time this customer has put pen to paper. The first time they make any mark on any document related to this vehicle. And psychologically, that matters more than most people realize. Once a person has written their initials on something, the decision is no longer entirely abstract. They have made a move. Now it feels real.

If you can get a physical signature or initial on something tangible, do it. A pen on paper is still the strongest commitment tool in the business. Whether your dealership uses a printed worksheet, a tablet, or a computer-generated form, the goal is the same. Get that mark. That small gesture is the moment a shopper becomes a buyer.

You can also add a second line below the statement: I will purchase and drive home today if we can agree on terms. If there are multiple decision makers, have each one initial it. This is not just paperwork. It is psychology. It is mental ownership captured on paper before you ever leave the table.

Now here is the part that separates good salespeople from great ones.

Stand up, take the worksheet, smile, and say: "Wish me luck. Let me go see what I can do."

Take about three steps toward the office. Stop. Turn around. Walk back and say, "Hey, just want to make sure of something." If my manager can make all of these numbers work, we have got a deal today, right?

They will say yes. They almost always say yes because they've just initialed the paper and are already there mentally.

Then say: and just between us, if something needs to move just a little to get this done, which of these boxes do you think you have the most flexibility on?

Let them answer. Listen carefully. What they tell you right now is the most valuable information you will receive in this entire process. You now know which number has room to move before you ever sit down with your manager. You walk into that office knowing exactly what you need to bring back to close the deal.

That question does two things at once. It confirms that the numbers you are about to fight for will actually close the deal. And it shows you exactly where the customer has room to move if the desk cannot reach where they want to be.

Then turn around and walk away with confidence. The customer feels good because you are going to fight for them. And you feel good because you know exactly what you are fighting for.

FROM THE FLOOR

I once had a customer who was negotiating a vehicle while his partner waited in the car. Every time we got close to a decision, he would say he needed to check with her first. So out he would go. Then back in. Then out again. Back and forth, back and forth. It was taking forever, and the lot was about to close.

Now I will be honest with you. This one is partly on me. I never once asked to meet the partner. Never suggested she come inside. Never walked out to the car to introduce myself. I just kept sending him back and forth like we had all night. That was my mistake, and I knew it the moment everything unraveled.

One of our newer salespeople needed to move the customer's car off the side lot so we could lock the gate. He asked the customer if he could borrow the key.

The customer handed it over without hesitation. Sure, he said. Go ahead. Just do not disturb Matilda. She is in the back seat. She will not bother you.

The young salesperson walked out to the car. Came back about a minute later. Face completely red. Did not say a single word. Just handed the key back and walked away like he had seen something he could not explain.

Matilda was a mannequin.

Full size. Sitting in the back seat of the car, they drove in. The whole time I was sending this man back and forth across the parking lot to consult with a mannequin. Two hours of negotiating. Back and forth to a department store display dummy named Matilda.

We did eventually get the deal done. And I will give the customer credit, Matilda never once objected to the numbers.

But the lesson I took from that night stayed with me for the rest of my career. Always ask early who else is involved in making this decision. Is there anyone else you would like to include in this conversation? It is one of the simplest questions you can ask, and it saves you hours of going in circles. Sometimes, the second decision-maker is a spouse. Sometimes it is a parent. Sometimes it is a trusted mechanic or a best friend on the phone. And apparently, sometimes it is a smoking hot mannequin named Matilda.

Ask the question. Every time. Before you spend two hours negotiating with someone who has to keep checking with the back seat.

"The Rule: Know what your customer cares about, and sell to that. Everything else is just noise."

CHAPTER 10

STEP FIVE: PRESENTING TO THE DESK

WORKING THE DEAL, READING the Room, and Knowing When to Call for Help

You have got the customer's commitment on paper. You have got the numbers they are working with. Now you go to the desk.

This is where many new salespeople check out. They hand the paperwork to the manager, stand around waiting, and return with whatever number they are given, without understanding what happened or why. That approach costs you money, credibility, and deals.

Understanding what happens at the desk and how to be effective in that process is what separates salespeople who occasionally get lucky from salespeople who consistently close.

Here is something that most training programs never tell you, and it comes from someone who has sat on both sides of that desk. The way you present a deal to your manager matters just as much as the numbers on the paper.

I have watched salespeople walk up to the desk and say something like: "Here you go. This guy has no idea what he is doing; he is being completely unrealistic. Good luck with this one." Then they slide the paper across and wait.

What they just did is hand the desk manager zero motivation to help them. Why would a manager put in the effort to work a deal for a salesperson who already wrote it off before they even tried? They might as well throw the paper in the trash. Or worse, they call in another salesperson with a better attitude and let them finish what you started.

You cannot start from a negative and expect a positive outcome. It does not work that way.

When you walk up to that desk, lead with opportunity. Hey, I think we have got something here. The customer is serious; they are committed. Here is where they are, and here is what I know about where they have room to move. Now help me close this.

That is the approach that gets a manager leaning forward instead of leaning back. You are not just dropping paper on a desk. You are selling your manager on the idea that this deal is worth their time and energy. Treat it that way, and you will be surprised how much harder the desk works for you.

What the Desk Manager Is Doing

The desk manager also called the closer, the desk, or the tower, depending on where you work. The desk, or the tower, is responsible for structuring deals that make financial sense for the dealership while still getting to a number the customer will accept. They're thinking about front-end gross (the profit on the vehicle itself), back-end potential (what finance can add), trade equity, and bank guidelines all at the same time.

When you present a deal, you're giving them the raw material. The vehicle, the trade, the customer's stated numbers, and the deposit or commitment you walked out with. From that, they'll structure a pencil, the first official offer you'll take back to the customer.

Your job in presenting the deal is to give them a complete picture. What did the customer say about the trade? What do they care most about: price, trade, or payment? What's their personality like? Are they flexible or dug in? Did you identify their buyer type? All of that context shapes how the desk structures the pencil, so give it to them.

Don't just hand them the four square and walk away. Talk to them. "She's a trade allowance buyer, that's her issue; she's been very specific about what she expects for her car. The payment, she's flexible on. But if the trade number isn't close to what she's expecting, she's gone." That kind of information changes how the deal gets structured.

Taking the Pencil Back

The first number the desk gives you is rarely the final number. It is the opening offer. It is designed to give the dealership room to negotiate while still leaving a path to a deal.

When you take it back to the customer, your job is to present it professionally and gauge their reaction. You are not defending the number. You are not apologizing for it. You are presenting it calmly, watching what happens, and gathering information.

All right, here is what I was able to put together. Then walk them through it. Vehicle price. Trade allowance. Down payment. Payment. Simple and clear.

Then stop talking. Watch them.

This is the same principle we talked about when delivering the down payment anchor, and it applies here just as powerfully. The first person who speaks after presenting that number loses. If you fill the silence, you have taken the pressure off the customer to respond. You have signaled uncertainty in the number you just put in front of them. Let it sit. Let them process it. Give them the space to react honestly without you steering them toward a response.

The customer's reaction in the next ten seconds tells you everything. Do they lean in or pull back? Do they nod or cross their arms? Do they ask a specific question or go quiet? Their body language is giving you data about where the resistance is. Use it.

If they push back on the trade, you now know for certain that you have a trade-allowance buyer. Go back to the desk with that specific issue and fight for the trade.

If they push back on the payment, you know your lever is term length, down payment, or price reduction.

If they push back on everything at once, you probably have more work to do on trust. Slow down. Ask some questions. Find out what is really behind it.

The Back and Forth

Multiple trips to the desk can be normal. It is not a failure. It is the process.

What you are doing in each trip is narrowing the gap. The desk comes down a little, the customer comes up a little, and somewhere in the middle is a deal both sides can live with. Your job is to keep the conversation moving without either side feeling like they are being played.

Be honest with the customer about where things stand. You do not have to reveal everything, but you also cannot be so vague that they lose confidence in you. I am working on the trade number. I hear you, and I am going back in to fight for it. It is better than disappearing for ten minutes and coming back with a different number and no explanation.

And between trips, do not leave the customer alone and silent. Come back to them. Check in. Offer them something to drink. Keep the connection warm. A customer who sits alone for fifteen minutes starts to feel forgotten. A customer who feels forgotten begins to feel manipulated. Neither one helps your deal.

Mandatory Turns Revisited

We covered mandatory turns back in Step Two. The same principle applies here at the desk.

If you have presented the numbers, given the customer every opportunity to commit, and you still cannot get them to initial the worksheet or agree to move forward, that is your signal. Do not keep grinding. Recognize the moment and act on it.

Depending on your store policy, this means one of two things. Either you bring your manager in to sit down directly with the customer, or you make a formal handoff to another salesperson who comes in fresh, with no assumptions or baggage from the previous conversation.

Either way, the goal is the same. A new voice, a new energy, and a fresh start on getting the customer across the line.

Do not take it personally. Do not see it as a failure. See it as a tool. The customer may need to hear the same thing from a different person before they believe it. That happens more than you would think. Use every resource available to you before you let a deal walk out the door uncommitted.

FROM THE FLOOR

I had a couple sit down with me who were engaged and happy through the entire process. The qualifying conversation went well. They found a vehicle they loved. The walkaround and test drive went smoothly. We sat down at the desk and worked through the four-square without much resistance. The numbers made sense. Everything was pointing toward a deal.

Then I slid the worksheet across for their initials, and they looked at each other.

We need to go home and think about it.

I did not panic. I backed up and tried to find where things had come apart. I went through each box with them. Which number are you most concerned about? Is it the price? The trade? The payment?

They looked at each other again. No, they said. The numbers are fine. We just want to think about it.

I reminded them that when they came in, they had told me they were ready to make a decision today. They nodded. We know, they said. We just have cold feet.

Cold feet. Not the numbers. Not the vehicle. Not the deal. Just two people standing at the edge of a significant decision and needing one more reason to jump.

Our store had a mandatory turn policy, not to a manager but to another salesperson. I went and grabbed a colleague, gave him the thirty-second version, and sent him in.

He sat down, introduced himself, and did not talk about the deal at all for the first few minutes. He found some common ground, got them laughing, and broke through whatever wall had gone up. Then he looked at them and said,

"Sounds like you guys found the right car at the right number." Sometimes you just need somebody to tell you it is okay to say yes.

They signed.

Sometimes a deal does not need a better price or a different vehicle. It just needs a different face, a fresh energy, and someone to validate what the customer already knows. That couple knew the deal was right. They just needed one more person to confirm it.

That is what a good turn does. It is not a failure. It is a tool. Use it.

Getting Outside Help

Sometimes the deal needs something you can't provide on your own. The customer is stuck, and you've run out of moves. The desk can't bridge the gap on paper. Everyone is dug in.

This is where a third party can break the tension.

When I was managing, a salesperson came in to tell me a deal was stuck. The numbers were close, but the energy in the room had gone flat. I sent in one of our other sales associates. Her only job was to pop her head in, ask if anyone needed coffee or water, and maybe crack a joke.

Five minutes later, I could hear them all laughing through the wall.

Five minutes after that, the deal was signed.

A laugh does more for a stalled negotiation than another trip to the desk. If the energy in the room has gone cold and you can't warm it back up yourself, get someone else to do it. There's no shame in that. That's just knowing your tools.

FROM THE FLOOR

I had a single woman who was trading in a car that her mother had left her. Her mother had passed away young, and this car had been her mother's. She'd driven it for fifteen years. Everything was agreed upon, numbers, financing, all of it. Finance was ready to sign the paperwork.

She went out to say goodbye to the car. And she sat in it for an hour, crying.

Finance was getting impatient. My manager was getting impatient. I went outside, knocked gently on the passenger window, and got in with her.

I didn't rush her. I just sat there with her for a while. Then I told her it was okay to cry, and that her mother's car had taken good care of her all these years and would take good care of whoever drove it next.

She thanked me, took a breath, and came inside.

We signed the paperwork. She drove home in a new vehicle.

Sometimes closing a sale has nothing to do with numbers. Sometimes it's about recognizing what this moment means to the person sitting across from you, and being human enough to honor it.

"The Rule: Know what you're walking into before you walk into the desk. Context closes deals. Numbers alone don't."

CHAPTER 11

STEP SIX: CLOSING THE SALE

MAKING IT REAL, MAKING IT Stick, and Getting Them to the Finish Line

You have done the work. The numbers are agreed upon. The customer is nodding. The energy in the room has shifted. Everything that needed to happen has happened.

Now comes the moment that most salespeople handle wrong.

They say something like, "Great, let me get the paperwork started." Or they disappear to find a manager. Or they sit back down and start explaining things that no longer need to be explained.

Do not do any of that.

Here is what you do instead.

The Handshake Close

Stand up. Walk back to the customer with a big smile on your face. Do not say a word yet. Stick your hand out in front of the primary buyer, man or woman, and wait.

They will shake it—every time.

The moment their hand meets yours, look them in the eye and say: "Congratulations, you just bought a car."

Then turn to the spouse—same thing. Hand out, eye contact, congratulations. If there are kids there, get them involved too. Shake their hands. Make it fun. Make it a moment.

Here is why this works. The moment someone shakes your hand and hears those words, the deal becomes real and public at the same time. It is no longer a number on a worksheet. It is a social commitment made in front of other people. Nobody wants to back out of something they just celebrated. Nobody wants to be the person who shook hands, smiled, and then said, "Actually, never mind."

The handshake does not just confirm the deal. It seals it emotionally in a way that paperwork alone never can.

Make It a Celebration

Do not be quiet about it. Let it be a moment.

Other salespeople on the floor will notice. Colleagues working their own deals nearby will feel the energy shift. Other customers in the showroom who are still working through their own decisions will see it and feel it too. A deal closing visibly and happily is contagious. It raises the energy in the room for everyone.

Think of it like ringing a bell. In a restaurant, when a server gets a great tip, they ring the bell, and everyone knows. It encourages other customers to do the same. A visible celebration of a deal closing does the same thing on a sales floor. It motivates your colleagues. It reassures other customers that people are making good decisions here today and walking away happy.

Make it a spectacle in the best possible way.

What Happens Next

Once the handshake is done and the celebration has had its moment, the delivery process begins. This is where your job shifts from selling to serving.

Finance needs to get the paperwork together. If financing is involved, it may need to be approved. That takes time. Your job during that window is to keep the customer comfortable, informed, and in the building.

Make sure the desk has everything they need before you do anything else. Driver's licenses. Trade title if applicable. Proof of insurance. Many states require that customers have liability insurance before they can drive a vehicle off the lot. If your customer does not have that arranged, help them get it sorted before they sit down in finance. Do not let it become a last-minute problem.

If your dealership has a service department, take your customer on a service walk. Introduce them to the service advisor, who will handle them going forward. Show them where the parts counter is. If there is a body shop, point it out. Let them know their new vehicle is being prepped for delivery and give them a realistic sense of how long the process will take.

A customer who knows what is happening and why is patient. A customer sitting in a waiting area with no information or contact is one who starts to feel forgotten. And a customer who feels forgotten starts to feel manipulated. Neither one is good for you or the deal.

Check in on them regularly. Think of yourself as their waiter during this window. You are not sitting with them every minute, but you are circling back consistently. Can I get you some water? Some coffee? Just wanted to let you know they are almost finished with the vehicle. You are keeping the connection warm and the experience positive all the way to the end.

Prospect During the Wait

While your customer is comfortable and happy and has nothing to do but sit and talk to you, pull out your notepad.

Ask them: of all your friends, family, and coworkers, who do you think is most likely to be in the market for a vehicle soon?

Let them think about it. Let them give you names. This is one of the best moments in the entire sales process to ask for referrals, because the customer is relaxed, feels great about the deal, and is sitting right in front of you with time to spare.

Let them know you pay referral fees. Keep it light. Keep it fun. I used to tell customers I had people who sent me so many referrals over the years that they never had to make a car payment. I just kept mailing them checks. It always got a laugh and made the point.

A happy customer who sends you one referral is worth more than ten cold ups off the lot. Use this time well.

FROM THE FLOOR

I spent an hour and a half with a customer who was happy with the price, the payment, and the vehicle. He just couldn't quite get himself across the line. Every time I thought we were there, he'd find another reason to hesitate.

I finally realized he wasn't looking for a different number. He was looking for someone to tell him it was okay to make this decision. He was a passive personality who needed reassurance more than negotiation.

I put my hand on his arm and said, "Let's go take one more drive. I want to make sure this is really the right fit for you."

We took the car out again. I drove past his neighborhood and suggested we park it in his driveway and see how it looked. A neighbor walked over and said, "Wow, that's beautiful."

That did it. We went back to the dealership, and he bought the car. He ended up sending me several referrals over the next year.

Some customers need a nudge. Some need a second test drive. Some need their neighbor to say it looks great. Read the person, not just the deal.

FROM THE FLOOR

One day, I was paged to the finance office while a customer was signing paperwork for a vehicle purchase.

The customer was a young mother with a newborn baby. She was struggling because the baby was squirming and crying while she was trying to review and sign the finance documents.

The finance manager looked at me and asked if I could help with the baby for a few minutes so the customer could focus.

I told the customer that I had raised three children and would be happy to help.

The mother smiled with relief, and as I went to grab the baby while she held it against her chest, I leaned in and carefully picked it up.

Unfortunately, in the process of trying to support the baby correctly, I re-alized very quickly that one hand was on the baby and the other hand was somewhere it absolutely should not have been.

Both the customer and the finance manager immediately froze and stared at me.

I turned about four shades of red in less than two seconds.

Trying to recover from the situation, I awkwardly explained that I thought I was reaching for the baby's bottom with my left hand while supporting the baby's head with my right hand.

Unfortunately, what I actually grabbed was not the baby.

There was about one second of complete silence.

Then both women completely burst out laughing.

At that point, there was nothing I could do except sit quietly in the chair, holding the baby, while looking as red as an apple.

Fortunately, the laughter completely relaxed the room, the paperwork got signed, and the deal was completed successfully.

"The Rule: If you've done the work, you've earned the right to ask. Ask directly, stop talking, and let the customer say yes."

CHAPTER 12

STEP SEVEN: FOLLOW UP

Where the Real Relationship Begins

Most salespeople think the sale ends when the customer drives off the lot.

They shake hands, wave goodbye, and immediately turn their attention to the next up. The deal is done, time to move on.

That mindset is one of the most expensive mistakes you can make in this business.

The moment a customer drives away in a vehicle you sold them, the sale is not over. It's the beginning of the relationship. And that relationship, how you handle it, whether you invest in it or ignore it, is what determines whether that customer ever comes back, and whether they send anyone else your way.

The salespeople who build real careers in this business, the ones who are still selling twenty years in and have customers who follow them from dealership to dealership, understand this. They treat the sale as the start, not the finish.

The First Call

Within twenty-four hours of a customer taking delivery, you call them.

Not to sell them something else. Just to check in.

"Hey, I just wanted to make sure everything is going smoothly with the new vehicle. Is there anything I can answer for you? Anything that feels unfamiliar or different? How did your family and friends like the new car?

Also, if you happen to know anyone else who may be in the market for a vehicle, remember, we do pay for referrals."

That call takes three minutes. And it accomplishes something that almost no other salesperson does: it tells the customer that you didn't disappear the moment they signed. You're still there. You still care. You're the professional who stays involved.

Most customers are mildly surprised by this call because they've been conditioned to expect that salespeople vanish after the transaction. When you don't vanish, you stand out. And standing out for the right reasons is exactly what builds a referral business.

Buyer's Doubt Is Real

Here's something that happens to almost every customer after a major purchase: buyer's doubt.

They drove home excited. They showed the car to their family. And then somewhere in the night, the second-guessing crept in. Did I pay too much? Did I get enough for my trade? Is this really the right vehicle? Should I have looked at one more option?

This is completely normal human psychology, and it has nothing to do with whether they made a good decision. It's just what brains do after committing significant money to something.

Your follow-up call addresses this directly, even without naming it. When you call to check in, you're implicitly reinforcing that the decision was sound. You're the professional who helped them through the process, and you're still standing behind it. That's enormously reassuring. It closes the loop on any doubt before it hardens into regret.

A customer who feels confident about their purchase tells others about it. A customer who second-guesses themselves tells others about it, too. Your follow-up call tips that balance in the right direction.

The Customer Who Never Bought

Follow-up isn't just for the customers who purchased. It's also for the ones who didn't.

A customer who came in, spent time with you, and left without buying isn't necessarily a lost cause. They might not have been ready that day. They might have needed more time to think. They might have been comparing a few options. If you gave them a good experience, if you were professional, knowledgeable, and pressure-free, they will remember you when they are ready to buy.

A follow-up call a day or two later: "Hey, I just wanted to reach out and see if you had any other questions after your visit. No pressure at all, I want to make sure you have everything you need to make the right decision."

Some of them will buy. Some won't. But all of them will remember that you called.

FROM THE FLOOR

I once had a customer I spent a good part of an afternoon with. Good conversation. Good test drive. We got close on numbers, but couldn't quite get there. He left without buying.

I gave him my card, thanked him for his time, and told him I'd love to help him or anyone he knew in the future.

I followed up that same afternoon with a call, just to check in and see if he had any other questions. He was gracious about it.

A few days later, I found out he was a community leader in his neighborhood and had mentioned his experience at the dealership and with me specifically at a neighborhood meeting that week.

Over the next two months, I sold five vehicles to people who lived in his neighborhood. Five sales from a customer I never closed.

I never sold him a car. I sold everyone he sent me.

The relationship matters more than the transaction. Always.

Managing Your Customer Bank

Back in the days before CRM software, we kept index cards. A card for every customer name, phone number, spouse's name, kids' names, date of birth, anniversary, what they bought, and when they bought it. Every piece of information that would help us reach out in a way that felt personal rather than generic.

The idea was simple: people do business with people who remember them.

When you call a customer on their birthday, that's memorable. When you reach out on the anniversary of their purchase, that's memorable. When you call to let them know a vehicle just came in that matches something they'd mentioned they were looking for, that's memorable. You're not just a salesperson. You're someone who pays attention.

Today, you have CRM tools that do most of the tracking automatically. Use them. Fill them in completely every time. Notes on the conversation, on what the customer cares about, and on anything personal they mentioned. That database is your future business.

The salespeople who build a real customer bank who invest in those relationships over the years eventually reach a point where they don't need as much lot traffic as everyone else. Their phone rings. Their past customers come back. Their referrals walk in asking for them by name. That's the career goal. Follow-up is how you get there.

How to Ask for a Referral

This is simpler than most people make it out to be.

You don't need a script. You don't need a formal ask. You need to be direct and genuine at the right moment.

When a customer is happy, when they're excited about their vehicle, when they've just told you how smooth the process was, when they're feeling good, that's the moment. "I'm really glad we could make this work for you. If you have anyone in your life who's thinking about a vehicle, I'd love the opportunity to take care of them the same way."

That's it. No pressure. No incentive program. No awkward referral card. Just a genuine ask at the right moment from someone who did a good job.

Customers who had a great experience want to share it. They're already thinking about who they know who needs a car. All you're doing is opening the door.

After the Sale Is Part of the Sale

I want to close this chapter with something that took me a few years to understand fully.

The way you handle the period after a sale, the follow-up call, the check-in, the birthday acknowledgment, and the referral ask is not extra work on top of your job. It is your job. It's the part of the job that most salespeople skip because it doesn't feel urgent. No customer is standing in front of you. There's no commission check on the line. No manager is watching.

But it's the work that compounds. It's the work that builds over months and years into something most salespeople never achieve: a business within a business. A customer base that generates its own momentum.

The salespeople who make the most money in this industry long-term are rarely the ones who were the most naturally talented or the most aggressive closers. They're the ones who took care of their customers after the sale and watched those customers come back, bringing others with them.

Do the follow-up. Every time. It's the easiest step in the process to skip, and the one that costs you the most when you do.

"The Rule: The sale ends when the customer drives away. The relationship starts there. Take care of the relationship, and the sales take care of themselves."

Chapter 13

CRM

Managing Your Customer Relationships From Index Cards to Artificial Intelligence

When I started in the car business in the late 1980s, my CRM was a box of index cards.

Three-by-five cards, handwritten, one per customer. Name, phone number, spouse's name, kids' names, date of birth, anniversary, what they bought, when they bought it, and any personal details they'd mentioned that I might use to connect with them later. That box sat on my desk, and it was, in every practical sense, my entire follow-up system.

When a customer's birthday came up, I pulled their card and made a call. As the anniversary of their purchase approached, I reached out. When a new model came in that matched something they'd mentioned wanting, I had their number right there.

It was simple. It worked. And the principle behind it that remembering people is how you keep them is exactly as true today as it was then.

The tools have changed beyond anything I could have imagined back then. But the principle hasn't moved an inch.

What a CRM Actually Is

CRM stands for Customer Relationship Management. At its core, it's exactly what it sounds like: a system for managing your relationships with customers. Who they are, how you found them, what you've sold them, when you last spoke, what they're likely to need next, and how to reach them when the time is right.

In a traditional dealership today, the CRM is software, usually a cloud-based platform accessible from your computer, tablet, or phone. Every customer interaction gets logged—every call, every visit, every email, every text. The system tracks where each lead came from, where they are in the buying process, and when they're due for a follow-up.

Done well, a CRM turns what used to be a box of cards into a living, searchable, automated database that ensures no customer falls through the cracks. Done poorly, which means filled in halfway, ignored between deals, or treated as a reporting burden rather than a tool, it's just expensive software collecting dust.

Most salespeople use their CRM poorly. That's actually good news for you, because it means that using it well is one of the easiest ways to separate yourself from the competition.

Why CRM Matters More Than Most Salespeople Realize

Here's a number worth thinking about: it costs roughly five to ten times more to acquire a new customer than to retain an existing one. That ratio holds across almost every industry, and the car business is no exception.

Every customer who bought from you is a future customer. They will need another vehicle. They may have a spouse who needs one. They have friends and family who are going to buy cars. If you stay connected to them professionally, consistently, without being annoying, you become the person they call when that moment arrives.

If you don't stay connected, someone else will. Or they'll walk onto a lot, not remember your name, and start the whole process over with a stranger.

Your CRM is the infrastructure that makes staying connected possible at scale. When you have fifty customers in your bank, you can probably remember most of them without a system. When you have five hundred, you can't. The CRM is what keeps every one of those relationships alive and active without requiring you to hold it all in your head.

The Core Functions Every CRM Should Do

Regardless of which platform your dealership uses, a good CRM should do the following things:

Store complete customer profiles.

Name, contact information, vehicle history, personal notes, family information, and communication preferences. Everything you'd have written on that index card, plus more.

Track every touchpoint.

Every call, email, text, and visit gets logged with a date and notes. You should be able to pull up any customer and see exactly when you last spoke, what was discussed, and the next step.

Set follow-up reminders.

The system should tell you who to call today. Not who you remember to call. The data says who needs a touchpoint right now, based on when they bought, where they are in the pipeline, or when their birthday falls.

Manage your pipeline.

Every lead should have a status: new inquiry, appointment set, visited, working a deal, purchased, lost, or long-term follow-up. Knowing where every customer is in the process lets you prioritize your time and energy.

Generate reports.

How many leads did you get this month? How many converted to appointments? How many appointments converted to sales? Where are deals falling out of your pipeline? Good CRM data answers these questions and tells you exactly where to improve.

Common Platforms in Automotive Sales

The automotive industry has several widely used CRM platforms across dealerships. Your store may already have one in place. If you're evaluating options or want to understand the landscape, here are the tools you're most likely to encounter:

VinSolutions is the most widely used in franchise dealerships.

A comprehensive automotive CRM that integrates with your DMS (Dealer Management System), your website, and your inventory system.

Strong on lead management, follow-up automation, and reporting. Most salespeople encounter this one early in their careers at larger stores.

DealerSocket Full-suite dealership platform

Combines CRM, inventory management, and digital retailing tools in one platform. Particularly strong for used car operations and stores that want everything in a single system.

Elead (now part of CDK Global) Enterprise-level platform

One of the longest-standing automotive CRMs is now integrated into the CDK ecosystem. Common at larger franchise groups and multi-rooftop operations. Strong phone integration and call tracking.

Dealer.com / Activix Boutique and independent options

Lighter-weight platforms that work well for smaller stores, independent lots, and buy here, pay here operations that don't need the full enterprise feature set.

HubSpot / Salesforce (with automotive integrations) Cross-industry platforms

Not built specifically for auto but increasingly used by forward-thinking dealerships, particularly in combination with AI tools. More flexible, often more powerful for marketing automation, but require more setup and customization.

The AI Revolution in CRM

Here's where things get genuinely interesting, and where the business is changing faster than most people in it realize.

Artificial intelligence has entered the CRM space, and it's not a gimmick. The tools available today, and those being released regularly, are doing things that would have seemed impossible even five years ago. If you're entering the car business now, understanding this landscape is part of being prepared for the profession you're actually walking into.

Here's what AI-powered CRM tools are doing right now:

Automated Follow-Up Sequences

When a new lead comes in from your website, a third-party listing site, or a phone call that gets logged, an AI-powered CRM can immediately trigger a follow-up sequence without you doing anything. Within minutes of a lead submitting their information, they might receive a personalized text message, then an email, then a follow-up text a day later if they haven't responded.

This matters because speed-to-contact is one of the single biggest predictors of lead conversion. Studies consistently show that a lead contacted within five minutes is dramatically more likely to convert than one contacted an hour later. When you're with a customer on the lot, you can't also be responding to every internet lead that comes in. The AI does it for you.

The key is that the best of these systems don't sound like robots. They're trained to communicate in a natural, conversational tone that feels like a person reached out. Some of them are genuinely difficult to distinguish from a human follow-up.

Lead Scoring and Prioritization

Not every lead is equally ready to buy. Some customers are actively shopping and ready to purchase this week. Others are six months away from a decision. Others are just browsing and may never buy.

AI-powered CRM tools analyze behavior signals to predict which leads are hottest right now. How many pages did they view on your website? Did they look at financing options? Did they return to the same vehicle multiple times? Did they open your emails? Did they click the link in your text?

The system takes all of that data, runs it through its models, and surfaces the leads most likely to convert today to the top of your queue. Instead of working your call list in random order, you're starting with the customer who visited your site three times yesterday and opened every message you sent. That's a very different conversation from cold-calling someone who submitted a form two weeks ago.

Automated Appointment Reminders and Confirmations

We covered appointment reminders in the script section. AI CRM tools handle this automatically. The system sends a text confirmation the day after the appointment is booked, another reminder the day before, and a check-in the morning of. If the customer responds to reschedule, many platforms can handle that conversation automatically and find a new time without any human involvement.

This sounds impersonal, but it's actually the opposite. These touches happen consistently, at exactly the right time, every time, without relying on a salesperson to remember to do them manually. The customer gets a better experience because the follow-up never falls through the cracks.

AI-Powered Conversation Tools

Some of the most advanced tools now include AI assistants that can handle the first several exchanges with a new lead entirely on their own—the customer texts in with a question about a vehicle. The AI responds naturally, answers the question, asks a qualifying question or two, and attempts to set an appointment. When the conversation reaches a point that requires a human, it flags the salesperson and hands off the thread.

Platforms doing this in automotive today include:

Podium Messaging and AI communication

Strong text-based communication platform with AI response capabilities. Widely used in automotive for managing inbound texts and reviews simultaneously.

Conversica AI sales assistant

One of the original AI follow-up tools for automotive. Sends personalized follow-up emails and texts on behalf of the dealership, handles responses, and escalates hot leads to humans when they're ready.

Fullpath (formerly AutoLeadStar) AI data platform for dealerships

Connects dealership first-party data with AI to personalize marketing and follow-up at a customer-specific level. Strong for larger operations managing significant lead volume.

DriveCentric AI-powered automotive CRM

Built from the ground up with AI integrated into the core product rather than bolted on. Focuses on conversation intelligence and helping salespeople have better interactions with customers.

What This Means for You as a Salesperson

Reading all of this, you might be wondering whether AI is going to replace you. It's a fair question, and I want to answer it directly.

No. It's not.

Here's why. AI is extraordinarily good at consistency, speed, and volume. It will follow up with every lead within minutes, every time, without getting tired or distracted. It will send the right message at the right time without anyone having to remember. It will handle routine questions and appointment logistics without human involvement.

What it cannot do is sit across from a person and make them feel understood. It cannot read a customer's body language as they're about to walk away and know exactly what to say to bring them back. It cannot sit in a car with someone and ask about their family in a way that feels genuine because it is genuine. It cannot hold a woman's hand as she says goodbye to her mother's car.

The human part of selling the connection, the trust, the reading of people, is not going anywhere. What AI does is handle the mechanical parts of follow-up and lead management so that when you do engage with a customer, you're spending that time on what only a person can do.

The salespeople who will struggle are the ones who resist these tools or refuse to learn them. The ones who will thrive are those who use AI to handle the volume of work while focusing their energy on the human work.

That combination of AI handling the consistent mechanical follow-up, and you handling the genuine human selling is more powerful than either alone.

How to Use Your CRM Like a Professional

Regardless of what platform your dealership uses or how much AI is built into it, here are the habits that will make your CRM work for you rather than against you:

Fill it in completely, every time.

A CRM is only as good as the data in it. If you log a call without notes, the next time you pull up that customer, you have no idea what was discussed.

Spend two minutes after every interaction adding real notes. What did they say? What do they care about? What's their timeline? What's their buyer type? In the future, you will thank the present you every single time.

Set your follow-up tasks before you close the record.

Every customer interaction should end with a next step scheduled in the system. Call back in three days. Send vehicle options tomorrow. Check in after the appointment. If there's no task set, the customer will fall through the cracks.

Work your task list first thing every morning.

Before you look at new leads or check your email, open your CRM and see who you need to follow up with today. Those people already know you. They're easier to close than a cold lead. Work them first.

Never let a lead go cold without a decision.

If a customer has gone quiet after multiple attempts, don't just leave them sitting in your active pipeline. Make a decision: move them to a long-term nurture sequence, mark them as lost with a reason, or make one final direct attempt. A bloated pipeline full of dead leads makes it hard to see your real opportunities.

Use the personal notes field.

When a customer mentions their daughter just started college, their son plays basketball, they're planning a road trip, their dog is named Biscuit, write it down. When you call them three months later and ask how the road trip went, you become the salesperson they remember. That's the index card principle, powered by software.

FROM THE FLOOR

When I started in the late eighties, my entire customer database fit in a shoebox. By the time I was managing, we had dedicated software that tracked hundreds of customers, logged every call, and flagged every birthday. By the time I retired, the platform our dealership used could predict which customers were likely to be in the market for a new vehicle based on their purchase history, lease terms, and website browsing behavior.

In thirty-five years, I watched the tools go from handwritten cards to artificial intelligence. What never changed was this: the salespeople who used whatever tool they had consistently and thoroughly outperformed the ones who didn't. The tool didn't matter as much as the discipline.

Whether your CRM is a shoebox, a spreadsheet, or a platform with AI built into it, use it. Fill it in. Work it every day. The relationship is in the data, and the data only exists if you put it there.

"The Rule: Your CRM is your customer bank. What you put in is what you get out. Fill it in completely, work it every day, and let the tools handle the consistency while you handle the connection."

CHAPTER 14

SCRIPTS

Why You Hate Them, Why You Need Them, and How to Make Them Work

FROM THE FLOOR

Early in my career, I had a problem I didn't yet know about.

Someone had handed me a phone script when I started. I looked at it, decided it was the dumbest thing I'd ever seen, and quietly put it in a drawer. Reading from a piece of paper while talking to a customer? Sounding like a robot running through a checklist? I was personable. I could figure it out on my own.

So I did it my way. And my numbers didn't improve.

For a long time, I blamed everything around me. The inventory. The lot traffic. The customers. The manager. I had explanations for everything. The script was never on the list.

Then one evening, I was out with a friend who sold at another dealership. We got to talking about the business, and I mentioned how much I hated scripts. He laughed. Said he'd felt the same way when he started.

Then he said something that stopped me in my tracks.

"Just because we don't like something doesn't mean it's not good for us. The script isn't the problem. The problem is we're using it wrong."

He explained what he'd figured out: don't read the script. Study it. Understand what it's trying to accomplish at each step. Then throw the paper away and put the whole thing in your own words, your voice, your personality, so it sounds like you're having a real conversation, not someone running through a checklist.

I drove home that night thinking about how much time I'd wasted blaming everything except the one thing I could actually control.

I went back to the script. I studied it. I rewrote every line in my own voice. I practiced it out loud until I stopped thinking about it.

My numbers improved.

What a Script Actually Is

A script is not a performance. It's a framework.

It exists because there are specific things that need to happen in every customer interaction: the information you need to collect, the questions you need to ask, and the commitments you need to secure. A script is the map that makes sure you don't miss any of them. When you're nervous, when you're distracted, when a conversation takes an unexpected turn, the script is what keeps you on track.

The salespeople who sound like they're reading a script sound that way because they're reading a script. The salespeople who have truly internalized it, understand the purpose of every element, and have translated it into their own natural voice, don't sound scripted at all. They sound like professionals who know exactly what they're doing.

That's the goal. And it takes time, repetition, and the willingness to commit to the process.

The Key Elements Every Script Should Hit

Whether you're working a phone call, handling an internet inquiry, or talking to a customer who walked onto the lot, there are core elements that need to be covered every time. Here's what they are and why they matter:

The Greeting

Your name, the dealership name, and a warm opening. This sets the professional tone and tells the customer immediately who they're dealing with.

The Purpose

Find out why they're calling or what brought them in. On a phone call: What vehicle are they inquiring about? Did they see an ad? Are they calling about a specific vehicle in inventory? This tells you where to direct the conversation.

Contact Information

Name, phone number, email. Get all three. Every time. Even if the customer seems resistant. "In case we get disconnected, what's the best number to reach you?" is a softer ask that most people will answer.

The Appointment

Every phone script should be driving toward an appointment. Not a maybe, not a "come by whenever." A specific day, a specific time. "I have an opening Monday at five-fifteen or Tuesday at noon, which works better for you?" Give them two options, both of which are 'yes'.

Your Name and Location

Tell them your name again before you hang up. Ask them to write it down. Give them directions or a landmark. Make it easy for them to find you and ask for you specifically.

The Confirmation

Repeat everything back before you end the call. Name, appointment day and time, vehicle they're coming to see, your name, and the address. "All right, so I have you scheduled for Monday at five-fifteen to take a look at the F-250. You'll ask for [your name] when you come in. We're at 1152 South Main, across from the HEB. Does that work?"

Handling Phone Objections

On a phone call, customers will ask questions you're not ready to answer. How much is the car? What's my payment going to be? What will you give me for my trade?

Remember the principle from Chapter Nine: respond, don't answer. You don't have enough information yet to give accurate numbers, and giving inaccurate numbers is worse than giving none at all. Here's how that sounds in practice:

Customer: *"How much is the car?"*

You: *"The price on that vehicle is going to depend on a few things: your trade, any down payment, and what kind of financing you're looking at. What I want to do is get you in so we can look at the whole picture and make sure the numbers work for you. Can you come in on Monday at five-fifteen or would Tuesday at noon be better?"*

You've responded to the question, explained why you can't give a number yet, and immediately moved toward the appointment.

Customer: *"What are my payments going to be?"*

You: *"That's really what we need to sit down and figure out together. Payments will be based on your credit, your down payment, the term, and a few other factors. My job is to get you to a number that works for your budget. The best way to do that is to get you in. Are you available Monday evening?"*

Same principle. Acknowledge the question, explain why you need more information, and pivot to the appointment.

Customer: *"What will you give me for my trade?"*

You: *"Our appraisal team determines that based on the vehicle's condition, mileage, and the current market, but I can tell you we want to get you every dollar it's worth. The fastest way to find that out is to bring it in. When can you come by?"*

You've turned their question into a reason to come in.

What Management Is Actually Tracking

Here's something worth knowing about the world you're walking into, especially in dealerships that have invested in their sales systems.

Most modern dealerships record phone calls. Not secretly, it's disclosed and legal, but comprehensively—every incoming call, every outgoing follow-up. And in many cases, a manager or a third-party service is listening to those calls and grading them.

When I was managing, one of my regular jobs was reviewing call recordings each week. I built a spreadsheet tracking every salesperson. Did they get the customer's name? Phone number? Email? Did they ask about the trade?

Did they set an appointment? Did they confirm it? Did their tone sound confident and natural or nervous and robotic?

And I matched all of that data to their actual sales numbers.

The pattern was consistent. The salespeople who hit all the key points on every call, consistently, in a voice that sounded natural and confident, were always the top performers. Not sometimes. Always.

The ones who winged it had inconsistent results. Some good weeks, some bad weeks, no real pattern except that they couldn't replicate their success because they didn't have a process to replicate.

Consistency is the variable that separates average from excellent. The script is what makes consistency possible.

"The Rule: Don't read the script. Own it. Translate it into your voice, practice it until it's automatic, and use it every time without exception."

CHAPTER 15

CUSTOMER ONE

What Happens When You Step Into Their Shoes

In 1992, Chrysler Corporation did something unusual.

They launched a national initiative called Customer One, a comprehensive program designed to transform not just how their dealerships sold cars, but how every person in every dealership thought about the customer. The program was reported on by Automotive News at the time as one of the most ambitious customer satisfaction efforts in the industry, covering everything from dealer training to staff development to the fundamental culture of how Chrysler's franchise network interacted with the people who walked through their doors.

Phase One began in 1992 with a clear goal: change the mindset. Chrysler's customer satisfaction scores still lagged the industry average, and the company understood that the gap wouldn't close with better vehicles alone. It would close with better people, better trained and more customer-oriented, working as a team rather than a collection of siloed departments.

The training focused on two things: developing a more knowledgeable staff, and promoting team-based approaches to sales and service. Sales personnel worked with specialized reference guides and sales effectiveness materials covering marketing strategy, competitive comparisons, and vehicle-specific details. But the part of that training I remember most vividly had nothing to do with product knowledge.

It was an exercise in perspective.

The training ran over two days, structured so that every employee could attend without disrupting dealership operations. Not just the sales staff. Not just the managers. Every employee. The janitor. The parts counter. The title clerk. The lot attendant. The receptionist. The dealer principal. Everyone who touched the customer experience, in any way and at any level, went through the same program.

The Blind Spot Every Professional Has

Here is something that happens to everyone who gets good at their job, across every industry, without exception.

You forget what it feels like not to know what you know.

When you've been in the car business for a few years, the process feels completely natural. The steps of the sale, the four square, the desk, the finance office, it's all automatic. You move through it the way you get dressed in the morning: without thinking, without explaining, without even registering that any of it might feel unfamiliar or intimidating to someone experiencing it for the first time.

But to the customer walking through your door, none of it is automatic. The terminology is foreign. The process is opaque. The power dynamic is unfamiliar. They don't know what's coming next. They don't know what's negotiable and what isn't. They don't know whether they're being treated fairly or taken advantage of. They're navigating a situation that you find completely routine, and for them, it may happen once every five or ten years.

That gap between what you know and what they know is where most of the friction in customer interactions comes from. Not from bad intentions. Just from the professional's natural tendency to forget what it feels like to be on the other side.

Customer One was designed to close that gap.

The Paper Chain

One of the most memorable exercises from the training involved paper chains.

Every person in the room, remember, this was the dealer principal sitting next to the janitor, the sales manager next to the lot attendant, assembled paper chains. Connected loops, each one depending on the ones around it to hold the structure together.

Then, at a certain point in the exercise, someone deliberately broke a link.

The whole thing fell apart.

The point was immediate and impossible to miss. It doesn't matter how strong the other links are. It doesn't matter how experienced the sales team is, how beautiful the showroom looks, or how competitive the pricing is. One weak link, one employee who doesn't acknowledge a customer, one interaction that goes wrong, one moment where someone is made to feel unimportant, and the whole chain breaks.

The customer doesn't experience your dealership as separate departments. They experience it as one thing. One feeling. One impression. And if any part of that impression fails, it colors everything else.

The Spider Web

Another image from that training has stayed with me just as long.

Think about a spider web. The spider sits at the center, but the web extends outward in every direction. And here's the thing about a spider web: it's a communication system. When anything touches the web anywhere, a fly, a drop of rain, a finger, the vibration travels through every strand and reaches the spider instantly. The whole structure responds to a single touch.

That's what a dealership or any organization is supposed to be. Not a collection of separate departments doing separate things. A web where everything is connected, where information and care and accountability travel through every strand, and where every person feels the vibration of what every other person does.

When the janitor walks past a customer who looks lost and keeps walking, that vibration travels through the web. When the parts counter employee snaps at a customer who asked a "dumb" question, that vibration travels through the web. When the receptionist welcomes someone warmly and genuinely, that vibration travels through the web, too.

Every employee is a strand. Every interaction sends a signal. The question is what kind.

Exceeding Expectations Starts With Knowing What They Expect

The core philosophy of Customer One was simple: meet the customer's expectations at a minimum, and exceed them whenever possible.

But to exceed expectations, you first have to understand what those expectations are. And for most customers walking into a dealership, the baseline expectation is not very high.

They expect to wait. They expect to be pressured. They expect confusing paperwork and numbers that don't quite add up. They expect to feel like the salesperson is trying to get something from them rather than do something for them. Some of them expect to be talked down to, particularly women and certain groups who have experienced that in sales environments before. Some expect to be ignored. Some have been told by everyone they know that the car-buying experience will be unpleasant, and they've arrived braced for it.

When you understand that's the expectation they walked in with, the bar for exceeding it isn't actually that high. You don't have to do something extraordinary. You have to do the ordinary things: acknowledge them, treat them with respect, explain what's happening, and make the process feel manageable, and you've already exceeded what they expected to experience.

That's both a sobering commentary on the industry and an enormous opportunity for anyone willing to take it.

Small Gestures, Enormous Impact

Customer One reinforced something I'd been learning through experience but had never had articulated so clearly: the moments that define a customer's experience are seldom the big ones.

It's not the vehicle's price. It's not the interest rate. It's not whether the trade came in at the number they wanted.

It's whether anyone acknowledged them when they walked in. It's whether someone opened the door. It's whether the person who helped them knew their name by the end of the conversation. It's whether anyone looked at them like they mattered.

We instituted something at our dealership after the Customer One training that sounds almost too simple to be real: we empowered every employee, from the detail crew to the sales managers, to spend up to $100 per day to resolve a customer issue without asking anyone's permission. No approval required. No chain of command to navigate. If a customer had a problem and you could solve it for $100 or less, you solved it. Right then. On the spot.

The idea was that waiting for a manager to approve a solution often costs more in goodwill than the solution itself costs in dollars. By the time you've tracked down a manager, explained the situation, gotten approval, and come back to the customer, the moment has passed. The customer has already decided how they feel about the experience. A problem solved immediately, by whoever was closest, sends a completely different message.

FROM THE FLOOR

I wasn't even working the day this happened. I stopped by the dealership to pick up my paycheck and noticed a couple standing near the service counter looking frustrated. Their salesperson wasn't in. Nobody seemed to be stepping up to help them.

I introduced myself and asked what was going on. They'd recently purchased a used vehicle and discovered it hadn't come with an owner's manual. Small thing. But it mattered to them, and nobody had taken care of it.

I walked them over to the parts counter, ordered the manual, and told them the store would handle it. Five dollars. Done in five minutes.

That customer sent flowers to the dealership. Then he came back and bought three more vehicles over the years. His parts purchases alone were worth hundreds, possibly thousands of dollars over time.

All of it started with a five-dollar owner's manual and the decision to handle it right then instead of passing it along.

That's what Customer One was trying to teach. Not that big gestures don't matter. But those small gestures, done immediately and genuinely, are often the ones that last.

The Janitor Who Could Make Your Day

Here's a scenario straight out of the Customer One training.

A customer buys a used car. They're happy with the vehicle. They drive away satisfied. But a week later, they realize they only got one key for the car. They come back to the dealership, a little annoyed. Their salesperson is with another customer. The service counter has a line. Nobody jumps to help them.

Then Janet from the cleaning crew walks by, hears the customer venting to someone in the waiting area, and stops.

"I'm so sorry that happened. Follow me, let's go get you that key taken care of right now."

She walks them to the right place, makes sure it gets handled at no charge, and sends them on their way.

That customer is now a customer for life. Not because of the key. Because of Janet. Because someone who had no obligation to stop, who wasn't on rotation, who wasn't in the sales department, and wasn't being paid to handle that situation stopped anyway and made it right.

And every person who witnessed that interaction in the waiting room just watched the dealership do something they didn't expect. That's the viral moment that can't be manufactured with advertising.

Customer One was built on the understanding that this kind of service has to be possible at every level of the organization, not just at the top. When you empower your people, when you train them to see themselves as part of the customer experience, regardless of their job title, you create an environment where Janet can be the hero of that moment.

Treating Everyone Equally Is Not Optional

Customer One was also direct about something that the industry has historically not been great at: every customer deserves the same level of respect and attention, regardless of who they are or what they look like.

I've heard from women throughout my career that they felt talked down to in service departments. The technician explained things slowly, assuming they wouldn't understand. The salesperson kept steering the conversation toward the husband, even though she was the one asking questions and making the decisions.

I've heard similar things from customers of various backgrounds who felt that the level of attention they received was influenced by assumptions someone made before a single word was exchanged.

This is not only wrong. It's expensive. Every time a customer feels dismissed based on who they are rather than what they want, you've lost a deal and usually several future ones, because people talk.

The professional approach is straightforward: you don't know who you're dealing with until you talk to them. Treat everyone as if they're your best customer, because you genuinely cannot tell which one they are. Ask your questions, listen to the answers, and let the conversation tell you what you're working with. Everything else is an assumption that will cost you.

Open Five Minutes Early

One of the simplest and most memorable practical takeaways from Customer One was this: open your doors five minutes before you're supposed to.

It seems trivial. It isn't.

A customer who arrives at your service drive at 7:55 for an 8:00 appointment is already slightly tense. They got up early. They rearranged their morning. They're hoping this doesn't take longer than it should. When the door opens at 8:02 because the technician was finishing their coffee, that customer's tension goes up a notch. Not dramatically. But it's there.

Now imagine the same customer arrives at 7:55 and the door is already open. Someone greets them immediately. They feel early instead of waiting.

That two-minute difference is the difference between a customer who starts the interaction slightly relieved and one who starts it slightly irritated. And how a customer starts an interaction almost always shapes how it ends.

Open early. Unlock the door and welcome the first person through it. Tell them you're glad they came. Mean it.

These are not complicated ideas. They're just easy to skip when you're running on routine. Customer One was a two-day reminder that the customer is never on routine, and we can't afford to act like they are.

This Goes Beyond the Car Business

I want to be clear that everything in this chapter applies everywhere. Not just dealerships. Not just sales.

The neighbor you wave to in the morning. The person you hold the elevator for. The customer at whatever business you're in who looks slightly lost, slightly frustrated, and slightly like they're having a harder day than they wanted to have.

A simple acknowledgment costs you nothing. A genuine gesture of help takes maybe five minutes. And you genuinely cannot know how much that moment means to the person receiving it. Maybe it's nothing. Maybe it's the one good thing that happened to them that day. Maybe it's the thing they tell their family about at dinner. Maybe it's what sends them back to your business for the next twenty years.

Customer One was a Chrysler training program. But the lesson underneath it is older than any corporation and simpler than any curriculum.

People remember how you made them feel.

Everything else, the price, the process, the paperwork, fades. The feeling stays.

Make it a good one.

"The Rule: The customer doesn't know your process. They only know how it felt. Every person in the building shapes that feeling. Make sure yours is the right one."

CHAPTER 16

THE PSYCHOLOGY OF THE CUSTOMER

UNDERSTANDING HOW PEOPLE THINK, What They Fear, and How to Make Them Comfortable

Everything in this book comes back to people.

The steps of the sale, the four types of buyers, the scripts, the four-square, all of it is just a framework for guiding human beings through a process most of them find uncomfortable. The techniques work because people work a certain way. And the more you understand how people work, the more effective every other tool in this book becomes.

This chapter is about that. Not the mechanics of the sale, but the person on the other side.

They're Already Nervous

Before a customer ever sets foot on your lot, they've already had a conversation in their head about what this experience is going to be like. And for most of them, that conversation includes some version of the following: this is going to be uncomfortable, someone is going to try to pressure me, I'm going to get taken advantage of, I'd rather be doing almost anything else.

They've heard the stories. Their parents told them. Their friends warned them. Some of them have had bad experiences themselves. They arrive with their guard already up, and the first thing you need to do before any selling happens at all is bring that guard down.

Everything we've talked about in this book is designed to do exactly that. The calm approach, the pressure-free greeting, the service-oriented questions, and the test drive they led themselves into. All of it is architecture for comfort. When a customer feels comfortable, they open up. When they open up, they tell you what they need. When you know what they need, you can help them get it.

Start from the understanding that they walked in tense, and your first job is to change that.

They Don't Know the Process

Here's something most salespeople forget because they do this every day: the customer doesn't.

Most people buy a car every 3, 5, or 10 years. They don't know what a four-square is. They don't know what the finance office does or why the process takes so long.

All of that is completely opaque to them. And opaque feels threatening. When people don't understand what's happening, they assume the worst.

Your job is to guide them through the process clearly enough that nothing feels like a surprise. Not a full explanation of every step would be overwhelming. But enough transparency that they feel in control of what's happening. "What I'm going to do now is take this to my manager so he can look at the numbers and put together an official offer. I'll be back in just a few minutes." Simple, clear, no mystery.

You are the professional. They are the buyer. Your job is to make the process feel easy for them. That's what professionals do.

Status Means Nothing on Your Lot

I want to say something clearly that I've touched on throughout this book: the customer's status, income, education, or social position is completely irrelevant to how you treat them.

Not because everyone deserves equal respect, though they do. But because you literally cannot tell from looking at someone what they can afford. The guy in dirty work clothes might be worth millions. The woman in the rental car might have just sold her house and be ready to spend $10,000 today. The person walking the lot alone might be buying a car for an adult child. The couple who looks like they're barely getting by might have excellent credit and no debt.

I've sold vehicles to a former communications officer of Air Force One. I've sold to the presidents of large banks. I've sold a Viper to a man who looked like he'd just come from under one. Every single one of them wanted the same thing from me: a professional who knew what they were doing and made the process feel easy.

Status doesn't change what people need from you. Treat every customer as if they're your best customer, because you have no way of knowing which one they are.

Prejudging Costs You Money

Let me be direct about this because it's one of the most expensive habits in the business.

Salespeople who prejudge customers who look at someone and decide before the conversation starts that this person can't afford anything, won't be a serious buyer, or isn't worth their time, lose deals constantly. And they lose them in a particularly painful way: they don't know they lost them, because they never gave themselves the chance to find out.

I've watched salespeople walk past customers on the lot because they didn't look like buyers. I've watched colleagues dismiss someone in thirty seconds because of how they were dressed. And I've watched another salesperson, usually a newer one who hadn't yet developed the habit of judging, walk up to that same customer and close a deal.

Don't prejudge. Walk up to every person on that lot the same way. Do the process. Let the conversation tell you what you're working with. You'll be surprised more often than you expect.

Mirroring Done Right

Mirroring a person is often misunderstood.

Mirroring is not imitation. It's not repeating someone's slang back to them. It's not adopting mannerisms or speaking styles that feel theatrical. Customers see through that immediately, and it's insulting when they do.

What mirroring actually means is calibrating your energy, pace, and tone to match the person you're talking to.

If your customer speaks slowly and thoughtfully, slow down. Don't rush them with quick questions or fill their pauses. Match their rhythm.

If your customer is high-energy and enthusiastic, bring some of that energy to the table yourself. Don't be flat when they're animated.

If your customer is quiet and reserved, don't overwhelm them with volume or momentum. Give them room.

Suppose your customer is direct and businesslike, respect that. Don't try to warm them up with small talk they didn't ask for. Get to the point.

And if the situation calls for a little profanity, some customers talk that way; it's just their normal register. You can match that too, within reason and well out of earshot of anyone else. What the manager doesn't hear isn't always a problem. The goal is connection, and connection happens when the customer feels like they're talking to someone who's on their level.

The Reaction Is the Information

One of the most useful things I can teach you about reading customers is this: any reaction is useful.

When you deliver a trade figure, and the customer's jaw drops, that's information. When they nod slowly, that's information. When they go quiet, that's information. When they laugh, that's information. Even a blank expression is information; it tells you the customer is processing, or that you haven't given them enough to react to yet.

Your job is to watch for these reactions and interpret them. Not just hearing words, but reading the whole person.

I'll tell you a story that makes this point in a way I'll never forget.

FROM THE FLOOR

I had a rough night the evening before this particular sale. Stayed out too late. I wasn't quite at my best the next morning, which is never where you want to be walking onto the lot.

A couple came in. I did the meet-and-greet, introduced myself, and went to introduce myself to the wife. She moved her coffee cup from one hand to the other to shake my hand.

For reasons I still cannot fully explain, the words that came out of my mouth when I shook her warm hand were: "Wow, you're hot."

Both of them stared at me.

I recovered as fast as I've ever recovered from anything in my life: "I'm so sorry your hand is hot from the coffee cup."

They both burst out laughing. And from that point forward, the conversation was easy. We had a connection, not the one I'd planned, but a real one.

I sold the car.

The lesson here is not to accidentally say something inappropriate and hope for the best. The lesson is that a genuine reaction, even an unexpected one, even a bad one, gives you a roadmap. Their laughter told me the wall was down. I followed that energy and closed the deal.

Read your customers. Watch how they respond. Let their reactions guide you.

People Want to Be Led

This is perhaps the most counterintuitive thing in this entire book, so I want to make sure it lands clearly.

Customers don't want to be pressured. But they do want to be led.

There's a significant difference. Pressure means forcing someone toward a decision they're not ready to make, in a way that overrides their judgment. That feels bad and creates resistance.

Leading means guiding someone through a process they don't fully understand, in a way that respects their judgment while giving them the direction they need. That feels like service. And most customers will follow a confident, trustworthy guide through a process they find unfamiliar because that's what they came for.

Remember: your customer buys a car every three to ten years. You do this every day. You are the expert in this room. When you act like one when you're confident, organized, knowledgeable, and clear about what comes next, customers feel safe following you. That's not manipulation. That's professional service.

The moment you forget that you're the professional and start deferring to the customer on process questions they don't know the answers to, the whole thing gets wobbly. Stay confident. Lead the way. That's what they need from you.

"The Rule: Understand the person before you try to sell them the car. Everything else flows from that."

CHAPTER 17

WHAT ANNOYS ME ABOUT SALESPEOPLE

*A*N HONEST CHAPTER ABOUT *the Habits That Poison This Industry and How to Be Different*

I've spent 16 chapters telling you how to sell cars.

Now I'm going to spend one chapter telling you what I can't stand about salespeople. Because after thirty-five years in this business, I have a list. And if you recognize yourself in any of it, that's not an accident. It's a warning.

I want to be clear: I love this industry. It gave me a career, an income, a life I'm proud of. I've worked with some of the best people I've ever known. But I have also watched the profession damage its own reputation, year after year, because of a handful of habits that too many salespeople either never examine or never bother to change.

The car salesperson stereotype exists for a reason. This chapter is about that reason.

They Lie

This is the one that bothers me the most, and it's unfortunately not rare.

Salespeople lie about inventory. They lie about the price. They lie about what's included in a deal. They lie about what the manager said. They tell customers the vehicle has features it doesn't have, that the warranty covers things it doesn't, or that a competing dealership is out of stock, even though they have no idea.

And here's what I want you to understand about lying in sales: it doesn't work. Not long-term. Every lie you tell is a bomb with a fuse you can't see. The customer goes home, discovers the truth, and you've lost them forever. Worse, they tell everyone they know. One dishonest deal can cost you ten future ones.

Beyond the practical damage, it's simply wrong. The customer is trusting you to help them make a significant financial decision. Lying to them is a betrayal of that trust. It's not a sales strategy. It's a character failure.

Be honest. If the vehicle doesn't have a feature they want, say so. If the numbers don't work, say so. If you don't know something, say you don't know and find out. Honest salespeople build reputations. Dishonest ones burn through customers until there are no more to burn.

They Steal

I'm talking about stealing deals going around the rotation system, poaching another salesperson's customer, and taking credit for work they didn't do.

This happens in dealerships every day. A customer calls and asks for a specific salesperson who's with another customer, so a different salesperson "helps" them and then conveniently forgets to mention it later. A salesperson on a test drive with a customer gets back to find that someone else has already sat down with the family member who stayed behind. A manager pencils a deal in a way that cuts out the salesperson who did the legwork.

Stealing deals destroys team culture. It creates an environment where nobody trusts anyone, where energy is spent watching your back rather than working with customers, and where good salespeople eventually leave because it's toxic. I've seen entire sales floors fall apart because of this culture.

Don't be part of it. Respect the rotation. Respect your colleagues' customers. If you're not sure whether a customer belongs to someone else, ask. The two minutes it takes to find out is worth far more than the commission you'd lose if you got it wrong.

They Badmouth the Dealership

This one never ceases to amaze me.

A customer is sitting at your desk, and the salesperson starts complaining. The manager is unreasonable. The inventory is terrible. The prices are too high. The finance office is a nightmare. I'm trying to help you, but my hands are tied.

What exactly do they think this accomplishes? The customer's confidence in the dealership drops immediately. Their confidence in the salesperson drops right behind it. If the person trying to sell you something tells you not to trust the organization they work for, why would you buy anything?

Beyond the practical damage, it's disloyal. This organization is paying you to represent it professionally. If you have genuine problems with how things are run, take them to management. Talk to the owner. Find another job if it's that bad. But don't weaponize the customer's trust against the business that's paying your commissions.

Early in my career, I made a deliberate decision to speak positively about every dealership I worked for, not to my managers as a performance metric, but to my coworkers, to customers, to anyone who might carry those words somewhere. Not because everything was perfect. But because I understood that my reputation was tied to the reputation of the place I worked, and I wasn't willing to poison either one.

That decision, more than any technique I learned, is what kept me employed, promoted, and trusted for thirty-five years.

They're Greedy in the Wrong Ways

Let me make a distinction here, because greed in sales is complicated.

Being focused on your income is not only acceptable, but it's appropriate. You are in a commission-based profession. Making money is the point. You should be paying attention to gross, to volume, to your monthly numbers. That's not greed. That's running your business.

But the kind of greed I'm talking about is the kind that makes a salesperson chase every dollar at the expense of the customer's trust by packing a deal too much with products the customer doesn't need and didn't ask for, and refusing to negotiate fairly because they want to protect every last dollar of gross. Rushing a customer through the process because they see the next up walking onto the lot, and they want to get there first.

This version of greed is short-sighted and self-defeating. The customers who feel taken advantage of don't come back. They don't send referrals. They leave bad reviews. They tell their neighbors.

The salespeople I've watched build real long-term careers understood something that the greedy ones don't: taking care of the customer and making money are not in opposition. They're the same thing, just measured across different time horizons. A fair deal today becomes a repeat customer in three years and three referrals in between.

They Take It Out on Customers

This one, I have zero tolerance for.

I've seen salespeople argue with customers. Get into it verbally over nothing. Talk down to people. Make sarcastic remarks under their breath. In my years in this business, I have seen salespeople get into physical altercations with customers on the lot.

None of that is acceptable. Not once. Not under any circumstances.

Customers can be difficult. Some of them are rude. Some of them negotiate in bad faith. Some of them are having a terrible day and taking it out on whoever is in front of them. You are not required to enjoy any of that. You are required to remain professional throughout it.

If a situation escalates to a point you can't manage professionally, you get your manager. That's what they're there for. But you do not engage. You do not escalate. You do not win an argument with a customer, ever, because even if you're right, you lose. Every person watching that interaction is now someone who will never buy from you.

The Disneyland Principle applies here just as much as anywhere. You're on stage. Stay in character. The character is a professional.

They Don't Respect Their Own Profession

Here's the thing underneath all of the above that I find most frustrating.

A lot of salespeople don't take what they do seriously enough to do it well.

They show up unprepared. They don't know their inventory. They don't practice their scripts. They don't follow up. They treat the job as something they're doing until something better comes along, and then they're surprised when they don't succeed at it.

Selling is a profession. It requires skill, discipline, knowledge, and practice, just as any other profession does. The people who treat it that way build careers; the people who don't cycle through jobs and wonder why nothing ever sticks.

I'm telling you this because you picked up this book. That means you're taking this seriously enough to study it, which puts you ahead of a significant portion of your competition before you've sold a single car.

Keep that attitude. Protect it. This industry will reward it.

FROM THE FLOOR

I want to close this chapter with the story I mentioned at the very beginning of this book, because it illustrates an important distinction between the people who last in this business and those who don't.

When I first started at that Dodge dealership, the manager who hired me renamed me Ed. He ran a tough floor. The culture was competitive, sometimes cutthroat. Some salespeople stole deals, who bad-mouthed management, who showed up doing the minimum, and complained when their checks reflected it.

I made a different decision. I worked longer hours than most people around me. I didn't steal deals. I didn't complain publicly. When things were hard, I kept my head down and kept working. When things were good or bad, I kept showing up the same way. I committed to the process and to the dealership, even when it wasn't easy.

Salespeople came and went. I stayed. And the longer I stayed, the more I learned. The more I learned, the better my numbers got. The better my numbers got, the more the management trusted me. The more they trusted me, the more responsibility I was given.

A few years after the man renamed me, Ed, on my first day, I was his boss. We're still good friends.

The lesson isn't that loyalty alone gets you promoted. The lesson is that consistency, professionalism, and the willingness to do the job right, even when no one's watching, compound. They build into something that a clever shortcut never can.

Be the kind of salesperson this industry needs more of. There's plenty of room at the top for those who do it right.

"The Rule: Be the salesperson you'd want to buy from. Everything else follows from that."

CHAPTER 18

MOVING UP

How Salespeople Become Managers and What Changes When They Do

Nobody handed me a promotion.

In thirty-five years in this business, every step up I took was something I either created for myself or earned by being the person the dealership couldn't afford to leave where I was. That's not a complaint, it's just how this industry works. Management positions don't open on a schedule. They don't come with a clear application process. And they don't always go to the most qualified person in the room.

What I can tell you is how I got there. And more importantly, what I learned along the way that might save you some of the time and frustration it cost me.

The First Ten Years

I spent roughly ten years as a salesperson at the same Dodge dealership where I started. Ten years is a long time to stay in one place, and people sometimes ask me why I didn't move around more. The answer is simple: I was learning. Every year I stayed, I learned something new about the business, about customers, about inventory, about how deals get structured, about what managers are actually thinking when they pencil a car.

For most of that period, formal training was almost nonexistent. We didn't have the systems that dealerships have today. Chrysler Corporation had a training office in Portland where you could go work through some material on disks, yes, actual disks, but it didn't amount to much in practical terms. What training existed in the store was informal, inconsistent, and largely dependent on whether the person next to you felt like sharing anything useful.

About halfway through my time as a salesperson, the dealership started doing weekly formal training sessions. That's when things began to click more consistently. The exercises from those sessions are the foundation of everything in this book and in the micro series. Real, structured training even late in the game made a measurable difference.

But the bigger shift came from something else entirely.

The Promotion I Didn't Get

After a couple of years on the floor, a sales manager position opened up. I wanted it. I believed I'd earned it. I had the numbers, the experience, and the team's respect.

I didn't get it.

The owner's son, who was running new car sales at the time, had someone else in mind. Someone who ran in the same social circles, who had a relationship with the family. The position went to that person instead.

I'm not going to pretend that didn't sting. It did. And if I'm being honest, my first instinct was to leave. Find somewhere that recognizes what I bring to the table. A lot of salespeople make that move, and sometimes it's the right call.

But I made a different decision. I decided that if the front door were closed, I'd find a side door.

Creating My Own Path: Leasing

Around that time, I started noticing something. Other dealerships and sales reps I talked to kept asking whether we were doing any leasing. The answer was always no; our finance department was resistant, and without management support, nothing was going to change through the normal channels.

So I went around the normal channels.

I took a couple of days off, drove out to meet with a sales rep from a leasing company, paid him a few hundred dollars out of my own pocket, and spent two days shadowing him. He taught me how leasing worked, who it was right for, and how to present it to customers in a way that made sense to them. I came back to the dealership with a proposal.

My manager's response was essentially: fine, set up a desk and see what you can do.

The finance department was not happy. I was cutting into what they considered their territory, and they made that clear. They refused to help me program the contracts into the system, so I learned to do them by hand. They refused to help me present leasing to customers, so I learned to do that myself, too. For a while, it was a one-person operation operating out of a desk wedged between two showrooms, with no support from the people who should have been natural allies.

But it worked.

FROM THE FLOOR

The very first vehicle I leased was a Dodge Viper.

A man came into the dealership in dirty work clothes, grease on his hands, clearly having just come from a physical job. He was looking for a part for an older Dodge he was working on. On his way out, he said, half to himself, that he'd probably buy a Viper if he could get one at MSRP.

The other salespeople standing around kind of laughed it off. I overheard it. I told him I thought I could handle that.

He said, "Let's do it."

We went to my desk, ordered the car. When it came in, I went to his office to sign the paperwork. His office was on the top floor of a nine-story manufacturing plant downtown, an immaculate penthouse suite. Turns out he and his brother owned the company. They manufactured high-end bedding for Nordstrom's, Foley's, Dillard's, and Neiman Marcus. His brother ran the advertising and marketing division out of New York.

He leased the Viper. I made a commission on both the front end of the deal and the back-end lease money that the finance department had been leaving on the table by refusing to offer leasing.

It solidified everything. There was a market here. It just needed someone willing to find it.

From Leasing Manager to Fleet Manager

Once the leasing program was producing results, the dealership's position on it changed quickly. The finance department, the same people who had refused to help me and resented the whole operation, suddenly wanted to know why they weren't getting a piece of the back-end money. Management started paying attention to the numbers.

Around that same time, the dealership's fleet manager's assistant moved to a different position. They moved me into those roles: fleet manager assistant and official leasing manager. Now, any salesperson who ran into a customer interested in leasing or couldn't close on payments would bring me in. I became a resource for the entire sales team rather than just another salesperson working the floor.

That shift from individual contributor to someone the team depended on was the first real step toward management. I hadn't been given an official management title. But I was functioning in a management capacity, solving problems for other salespeople, and being trusted with deals that needed a different approach.

Eventually, I turned the leasing operation over to the finance department when I moved up. They'd finally come around to wanting it. By then, I was already moving toward the next thing.

Learning to Buy Cars: The Auctions

The dealership was growing. We'd purchased the Chrysler Jeep franchise, and eventually, the Ram truck branched out as its own manufacturer. A larger operation meant more inventory, more complexity, and more opportunity for someone willing to learn the parts of the business most salespeople never touch.

The used car manager started taking me to auctions, not as a passenger, but as an apprentice. Over the course of about a year, we traveled to auctions all over the Pacific Northwest. Washington State, California, Nevada, Las Vegas, New Mexico, Arizona, Montana, Idaho. I learned how to evaluate a vehicle at a glance. How to read condition reports. How to understand what the market would bear for a given make and model in a given region. How to bid without overpaying and how to walk away when the number didn't make sense.

This was a completely different education from anything I'd gotten on the sales floor. The auction is where you learn the real economics of used-car inventory: what vehicles are worth, what they cost to recondition, and what margin the dealership needs to make the math work. Understanding that side of the business made me dramatically more effective at the desk, because I understood the numbers from both ends.

After about a year of that apprenticeship running alongside the leasing operation and the fleet position, the used-car manager stepped away, and the position came to me. I became the official used car manager.

The Desk: Where the Real Education Happens

Managing used cars meant I was now at the desk, in the manager's position, who structures deals, pencils numbers, and makes the calls that salespeople bring their customers to the floor, hoping to get approved.

I want to spend a moment on this because if you're a salesperson reading this book, understanding what's happening on the other side of that desk will change how you present deals.

When a salesperson walks in with a four-square and a customer commitment, the desk manager is not just looking at numbers. They're evaluating the whole picture. Is this customer real? Did the salesperson do the work? Is the trade figure realistic? What's the customer's buyer type? Where is there room to move?

The salespeople who present deals well, who give the desk real context, who know their customer's type, who commit to hand, get better results from the desk. Not because managers play favorites, but because good information produces good decisions. When a salesperson walks in and says, "She's a trade allowance buyer, that's the whole issue, the payment she's flexible on," that tells the manager exactly how to structure the pencil.

When a salesperson walks in with a vague summary and no deposit or commitment, the manager has almost nothing to work with, and the deal stalls. The customer waits. Momentum dies.

Knowing this from the desk side is one of the most valuable things I can share with you. Every time you present a deal, think about what the manager needs to make a good decision. Give them that. Your closing rate will improve noticeably.

General Sales Manager

Eventually, the new car manager resigned. The dealership was at a point where consolidating the management structure made sense, and I was the person who knew every part of the operation, sales, leasing, fleet, used cars, auction buying, and desking deals. I became not just the used-car manager but also the General Sales Manager, overseeing the entire sales operation.

After many years of dedication and hard work, I went from walking through the door as a green salesperson named Ed to eventually running the sales floor.

What Moving Up Actually Requires

Looking back at that arc from green salesperson to General Sales Manager over twenty-five years, here's what I can tell you about how it actually happens:

It doesn't happen on a timeline. There is no promotion schedule in this business. You don't get reviewed every year and bump up a grade. Opportunities appear when they appear, often when someone leaves or when a new need emerges. Your job is to be ready when they do.

It happens through visibility, not just performance. Numbers matter. But management also promotes people they trust, people they depend on, people who are already functioning at the next level before they have the title. If you want to be a manager, start thinking like one before you're asked to. Take ownership. Solve problems. Be the person who makes the team better, not just yourself.

It sometimes requires creating your own path. The leasing opportunity didn't exist at my dealership. I went out and created it. When the front door to the sales manager position was closed, I found a side door. The car business rewards initiative in a way that very few industries do because it's a results business. If you produce results, eventually someone will want to give you more responsibility.

It requires patience and a very long memory. I stayed at one dealership for twenty-five years. That kind of loyalty is rare today, and I'm not necessarily saying it's the right choice for everyone. But there is something to be said for depth over breadth for knowing one operation inside and out, for building relationships that compound over years, for being the person who's still there when everyone else has moved on.

And it requires never stopping learning. In every role I moved into, I treated it as a new apprenticeship. Leasing. Fleet. Auctions. Used car management. Desking. Each one added a layer of understanding that made the next role possible. The salespeople who move up are almost always the ones who are curious about the parts of the business that aren't technically their job yet.

A Note on the 2008 Crash

After twenty-five years at that dealership, my wife and I decided to leave and open our own used-car lot. We did some buy-here-pay-here operations alongside traditional sales. I had the auction experience to buy inventory, the financing knowledge to handle our own deals, and the management experience to run the operation.

Then 2008 happened.

The financial crisis hit the car business across the board. Credit dried up. Customers disappeared. Dealerships that had been open for decades closed within months. We took a significant hit and eventually stepped back from the operation for a few years.

I tell you this not as a cautionary tale but as a reality check: the car business, like every business, is not immune to forces outside your control. Markets shift. Economies contract. Things that were working stop working through no fault of your own.

What I had when the crash came was thirty-plus years of accumulated knowledge and experience that nobody could take away. When I came back to the business a few years later, this time in the buy-here, pay-here space, that foundation was what I built on.

We'll talk about that world in the next chapter.

"The Rule: Moving up is not given. It's built deal by deal, role by role, year by year. Stay ready, stay visible, and create your own path when the obvious one is closed."

CHAPTER 19

BUY HERE PAY HERE

A Different World, Same Respect, Different Rules

Everything in this book up to this point has been built around the traditional dealership model. New cars, used cars, franchise stores, independent lots, the kind of operation where a customer comes in, you work the seven steps, and a bank or credit union somewhere approves the loan and takes it from there.

Buy here, pay here is something else entirely.

I spent the last decade of my career in BHPH, working as a finance manager, sales manager, and eventually general manager for a national franchise operation with multiple locations. Unlike a traditional dealership, everything in the BHPH environment is handled in-house, from the sales process to underwriting and financing. It is a completely different side of the car business.

I'm giving you a chapter on it here because if you end up in this world and a lot of people do, especially early in their careers, you need to understand what you're walking into. It's not better or worse than traditional retail. It's different. And different requires a different mindset.

I'll also be writing a dedicated micro-book series on BHPH in detail: one for salespeople, one for portfolio managers, and one for underwriters. This chapter is the introduction. The full education comes later.

What Buy Here Pay Here Actually Is

The name says it all. The customer buys the car there and makes their payments there. No outside bank. No credit union. No third-party lender in another state. The dealership is the lender. They own the loan, they collect the payments, and they absorb the risk.

Customers who come to BHPH are those who cannot be approved through traditional financing channels. Bankruptcies, repossessions (sometimes multiple), collections, medical debt, poor credit decisions, and job instability. Whatever the reason, the mainstream lending world has said no to them. BHPH says yes, under specific conditions and at a price that reflects the risk.

That price is visible in two ways. First, interest rates are significantly higher than those for conventional financing because the risk is higher. Second, the vehicles themselves are priced above what you'd see at a traditional used car lot for similar inventory again, because the dealership is absorbing a risk that a bank would normally carry.

This is not predatory by design. It is simply the economic reality of operating a high-risk lending business. When a dealership finances customers in-house, a percentage of loans will not perform as expected. Because of that risk, pricing and loan structures must account for the portfolio's overall health and sustainability. That is simply part of the business model.

Understanding this doesn't mean you exploit it. It means you can explain it honestly to customers who ask why the price or rate is what it is. Honest answers build trust, even when the news isn't what the customer was hoping for.

The Inventory Is Different

At a traditional dealership, you're working with a range of vehicles: new, certified pre-owned, late-model used. The inventory at a BHPH lot is typically older and higher mileage. It has to be, because the customer base can only support a certain monthly payment, and the deal has to pencil within that constraint.

This creates a real operational challenge: older, higher-mileage vehicles are more prone to mechanical issues. And when a customer in financial distress hits an unexpected repair bill on top of a car payment, the odds of them staying current on that payment drop sharply. The dealership I worked for understood this, which is why every vehicle in our franchise came with a warranty covering the powertrain and most major operating components. That warranty wasn't charity; it was risk management. A customer who can get their car fixed is a customer who keeps making payments.

Not every BHPH operation offers warranties. Suppose you go to work for one that doesn't understand that the lack of a warranty is going to be a factor in customer relations, repossession rates, and the overall health of the portfolio. It matters.

The Process Is Different

In a traditional dealership, the sequence is: meet the customer, find a vehicle, demo it, test drive it, establish the numbers, close the deal, send them to finance. The vehicle comes first. The financing gets figured out after.

In BHPH, that order is often reversed.

When a customer walks onto a BHPH lot, one of the first things you want to do after the meet-and-greet, which is exactly the same as anywhere else, is get them inside to go over the program. Not the cars. The program.

What does this dealership offer? Is there a warranty? Do they report to the credit bureaus (which matters enormously to a customer trying to rebuild their credit)? Will the customer have a chance to meet with the person making the financing decision? What does the approval process look like?

These questions matter to your customer before they fall in love with a vehicle. Because if they get attached to a car and then find out they don't qualify for it, or that the terms aren't what they expected, you've created a disappointment that damages the relationship. Get them oriented to the program first. Then work toward the vehicle.

Order of operations

Traditional: Vehicle first, financing second.

BHPH: Program orientation first, approval second, vehicle selection third.

Financing

Traditional: Third-party bank or lender. Dealership gets paid at closing.

BHPH: In-house. The dealership owns the loan and collects every payment.

Negotiation

Traditional: Expected. Price, trade, payment, and terms are all in play.

BHPH: Minimal. Prices are generally set. Down payment is the primary lever.

Customer profile

Traditional: Range from excellent credit to moderate risk.

BHPH: High risk. Traditional financing is not available to them.

Inventory

Traditional: New, Certified Pre-owned, and varied uses.

BHPH: Primarily older, higher-mileage used vehicles.

The Underwriting Interview

One of the most distinctive aspects of BHPH, and one of the things that genuinely helps customers when done right, is the underwriting interview.

In traditional financing, the approval decision is made by a bank's computer algorithm, which analyzes a credit score or the finance company's buyer. The customer never speaks to anyone making the decision. The credit score and customer payment history help make the decision.

In BHPH, especially in better-run operations, customers often have the opportunity to meet face-to-face with the underwriter or portfolio manager. This is as close to a job interview as anything in the car business. The underwriter is trying to answer two questions: can this customer afford to make this payment, and will this customer be willing to make this payment even when things get hard?

Income documentation, expenses, and basic math answer the financial ability question. The conversation addresses the willingness-to-pay questions.

I've seen customers come in with genuinely difficult financial situations who got approved because their attitude and honesty during the interview communicated that they would do everything in their power to keep their commitment. I've also seen customers with slightly better situations get declined because something in the conversation raised concerns about how they'd respond the first time a payment was inconvenient.

One exchange that always stuck with me: I once had a customer who, when asked what they would do if they couldn't make a payment one month, said, "I just won't pay it. You can come pick up the car if you want." That's an honest answer, and I respect it. But I wasn't going to approve that loan.

Then I had another customer in a genuinely rough spot who said, "I'd donate blood if I had to. I'd call my uncle. I'd figure something out. I am not losing this car." That person got approved.

The interview reveals character. Character predicts outcomes.

Your Role as a Salesperson in BHPH

As a BHPH salesperson, your job is different from your counterpart at a traditional store in one important way: you are not trying to close a sale. You are trying to get the customer through the approval process.

That distinction matters. In traditional sales, your energy goes into building desire for the vehicle and working the numbers. In BHPH, your energy goes into helping the customer understand the program, gathering accurate information for the application, and preparing them for the underwriting interview.

That last piece is critical. You cannot coach the customer on what to say; that's coaching, and it backfires every time. But you absolutely can coach them on how to present themselves. Tell them the truth: this interview is like a job interview. Be honest about your situation. Be clear about your income and your expenses. Be ready to explain what happened with your credit and what's changed since then. Show them who you are, not just what your score says.

Customers who go into that interview prepared and honest have a significantly better experience than those who go in defensively or who try to hide things. Help them help themselves.

FROM THE FLOOR

The hardest adjustment when I moved from retail into buy here pay here management wasn't the customers. It wasn't the inventory. It wasn't even the financing structure.

It was my own brain.

In retail, everything I'd been trained to do was about maximizing volume and gross. Sell as many cars as possible. Push the trade number. Grow the gross. More deals, more money, bigger month. That mindset was so deeply wired into me after twenty-plus years that it ran on its own.

BHPH doesn't work that way. The operation I managed had a monthly sales goal of 35 units. The goal wasn't to blow past it. The goal was to hit it consistently. Go too far over, and you're adding too many accounts to your portfolio too fast, straining your collections staff, and taking on risk you can't manage properly. Go under, and the portfolio isn't generating enough cash flow to sustain the operation.

The first time my manager told me to slow down on approvals because we were ahead of goal, I looked at him like he'd said something in a foreign language. Slow down? We're selling cars. That's what we do.

He explained it patiently. In BHPH, every car you sell is a loan you now have to collect on for the next two to four years. The sale isn't the end of the trans-action. It's the beginning of a long-term financial relationship. Your portfolio is a living thing. You manage it like a business, not like a scoreboard.

It took me a few months to fully rewire my thinking about success. Once I did, everything else about BHPH started making more sense.

Vehicle Selection in BHPH

Once a customer is approved, the vehicles available to them are typically determined by the underwriting decision. Higher-risk customers qualify for lower-priced vehicles with larger required down payments. Lower-risk cus-tomers, those just barely outside traditional financing, may have access to a wider selection.

In the operation I worked for, we used a tiered system: level 1 was the highest risk, level 5 was the lowest. A level one customer might be looking at a ten-year-old vehicle with significant mileage and a short-term loan. A level five customer might be getting into something more in line with a traditional lender, with maybe a lower rate and a longer term, because they may have a better credit score, better work history, income, and a larger down payment.

The meet-and-greet, the qualifying conversation, and the vehicle presentation still apply here. Every customer deserves the same professional approach and the same respect. The difference is that you're working within a narrower set of options, and your job is to find the best fit within that set, not to push customers toward something they can't afford or don't need.

This is especially important in BHPH because your customers are often in genuinely precarious financial situations. Getting them into the right vehicle at the right payment is not just good salesmanship. It's the right thing to do. An overextended customer defaults, loses their vehicle, and ends up worse off than when they came in. That's bad for them and bad for the operation.

What BHPH Teaches You About People

Of everything I learned in ten years of BHPH, the most lasting lesson has nothing to do with financing structures or inventory management.

It's this: financial hardship does not define a person's character.

I've worked with customers who had catastrophic credit histories and turned out to be the most responsible, reliable, grateful clients I've ever encountered. I've seen people who made terrible financial decisions in their twenties become completely different people in their forties with steady jobs, stable families, and a genuine commitment to rebuilding.

I've also seen people who had no intention of keeping their word from the moment they signed.

The job of the underwriter and, to some degree, the salesperson is to learn to tell the difference. Not based on credit scores. Based on conversation, character, and the willingness to be honest about a difficult situation.

That skill, reading people at a deeper level, looking past the surface to what's actually there, is one of the most valuable things BHPH gave me.

It made me a better judge of character in every context, business, personal, everything.

If you end up in BHPH, even for a short time, pay attention to what it teaches you about people. It's an education you won't get anywhere else.

A Note on Respect

I want to be direct about something before we close this chapter.

BHPH customers sometimes get treated poorly. Not at every store, not by every salesperson, but it happens. And it's wrong.

These customers are in a vulnerable position. They need transportation. The mainstream system has turned them away. They're paying a premium for the privilege of a second chance. They deserve every bit of the same professionalism, honesty, and respect that you'd give a customer at any other kind of dealership.

In fact, they deserve a little extra patience. The process is more complex. The documentation requirements are more involved. The approval is not guaranteed. A customer who comes in hopeful and leaves rejected has still had an experience with you, and that experience, how it felt, whether they were treated with dignity, is what they'll remember and what they'll tell people.

Treat them right. Every one of them. That's not just the ethical position. It's also the business position. The BHPH world runs on reputation just as much as traditional retail does. Sometimes more, because the customer base is tighter and word travels faster.

As I mentioned, the deep dive into BHPH, the full sales process, underwriting, portfolio management, and collections, is coming in its own micro-book series. What I've given you here is enough to walk into a BHPH environment and understand what world you've entered. The rest is a subject that deserves its own dedicated treatment.

"The Rule: Same respect. Different rules. BHPH is not a lesser version of the car business. It's a more complex one."

Conclusion

Playing the Long Game

What This Business Gives You If You Give It Everything

We've covered a lot of ground.

Seven steps. Four types of buyers. The meet-and-greet, the walka-round, the test drive, the four-square, the desk, the close, the follow-up. Scripts. Psychology. Income management. Staying on stage. Doing it the right way, consistently, even when it's hard.

If all of that feels like a lot, I understand. It is a lot. But here's what I want you to hold onto as you close this book:

None of it is complicated. All of it is learnable. And every single piece of it becomes easier with practice.

What This Career Can Give You

I retired at sixty-four. No college degree. Started as a high school dropout who couldn't afford to dress well enough to get hired at the first two dealerships I tried.

The car business gave me thirty-five years of income. It gave me the skills to read people, build relationships, negotiate effectively, and manage teams. It gave me the foundation to open a life-coaching practice, to help my wife build her mental health practice, and to publish books that might help someone else avoid the hard lessons I had to learn on my own.

I own my home. I have no debt. I have money in the bank. I have a life I'm proud of.

I am not telling you that to brag. I'm telling you that because I want you to understand what's possible from a career that most people underestimate. This industry has an image problem, and some of that image is deserved. But beneath the stereotype lies a legitimate profession that rewards those who take it seriously with something very few careers offer: unlimited upside and the freedom to earn exactly as much as you're willing to work for.

What It Requires

It requires showing up every day, ready to work, with your head in the right place.

It requires following the process. Not when you feel like it. Not when the customer seems worth the effort. Every time, with every customer, the same way.

It requires managing yourself, your money, your schedule, and your reputation. Nobody is going to do that for you.

It requires being the kind of professional that customers trust and managers depend on. Not because someone is watching. Because that's who you've decided to be.

And it requires patience. This business rewards the long game more than almost any other. The salespeople who build real careers are not necessarily the ones who had the best first year. They're the ones who showed up for the second year, and the third, and the tenth, getting better the whole time.

A Final Word

I wrote this book because nobody handed me one when I needed it.

I walked onto that lot in the late eighties with no training, no guidance, and no real understanding of what I was getting into. I learned by making mistakes, losing deals, getting chewed out by managers, and slowly figuring things out one customer at a time. Some of those lessons cost me commissions. Some of them cost me confidence. A few of them nearly cost me my career entirely.

If this book helps one new salesperson avoid some of those mistakes, it was worth writing.

And if it helps you build the kind of career that, thirty-five years from now, you look back on with pride, the kind that gives you a home, a family, financial security, and the deep satisfaction of having mastered something genuinely difficult, then it was worth every word.

Now sell some cars.

Bruce Huddleston

Appendix

The Complete Script Guide

Professional Scripts for Phone, Text, Email, and Objection Handling In Your Own Voice

A reminder before you use any of these scripts: don't read them.

Study them. Understand what each line is trying to accomplish. Then put every word in your own voice until the structure is automatic and the delivery sounds like you're having a real conversation, not a salesperson running a checklist.

These scripts are frameworks. They cover the key elements that need to happen in every interaction: collect contact information, handle objections with responses, not answers, set a specific appointment, confirm the details, give them a landmark, and ask permission to text. Do all of those things consistently, in your own words, and your results will improve.

A note on appointment times: always offer quarter-hour slots. "I have an opening at 2:15 or Thursday at 10:45" sounds like a real calendar, not a generic placeholder. It tells the customer you're organized and their time matters.

Full script downloads, additional resources, and updates are available to readers at the website listed at the back of this book. Enter your email, and you'll receive the complete digital script library plus access to the full Car Sales Survival Series.

Script 1: Inbound Phone Call

Use when a customer calls in response to an ad, online listing, or general inquiry. Your goal: collect their information, understand their situation, and set a specific appointment.

GREETING

Thank you for calling [Dealership Name]. This is [Your Name]. How can I help you today?

Warm, clear, and professional. Say your name distinctly so they remember it.

COLLECT NAME

Before we get started, may I get your name?

Get the name early. Use it throughout the call. People respond when you use their name.

COLLECT PHONE

And what's the best number to reach you at, [Name]? Just in case we get disconnected, I want to make sure I can reach you.

Framing it as "in case we get disconnected" removes any feeling of being collected. It's practical, and they almost always give it.

COLLECT EMAIL AND ASK PERMISSION TO TEXT

Do you have an email address you'd like me to use for anything I send over? And would it be all right if I reached out by text as well? I find it's usually faster if I can send you the address, a pin drop for directions, and any information on the vehicle so you have it right on your phone.

Always ask permission before texting. Explaining why texting is useful, pin drops, directions, vehicle info makes it feel like a service, not an intrusion. Most people say yes.

UNDERSTAND THEIR SITUATION

Tell me a little about what brought you in today. Are you calling on a specific vehicle you saw, or are you in the early stages of figuring out what you're looking for?

Open-ended. Let them talk. The more they tell you, the better you can help them and the more invested they become in the conversation.

QUALIFYING FOLLOW-UP

What's most important to you in your next vehicle? And what are you currently driving?

Two questions that give you your buyer type and their trade situation without asking directly. Listen carefully to which one they talk more about.

HANDLE PRICE QUESTION RESPOND, DON'T ANSWER

That's a great question, and honestly, the best way for me to give you accurate information on that is to get you in. The price is going to depend on a few things: your trade, any down payment, and financing. I want to make sure I'm giving you real numbers, not a guess over the phone. What I can do is have everything ready for you when you come in so we're not wasting your time.

Never quote a price cold on the phone. You don't have enough information, and any number you give becomes an anchor that works against you. Redirect to the appointment.

SET THE APPOINTMENT

Based on what you've shared, I'd love to get you in so we can look at the right options together. I have an opening [Day] at [Time use quarter hours, e.g. 2:15 or 4:45], or [alternate day and time]. Which works better for you?

Always offer two specific options. Give them a choice between two yeses. Quarter-hour times sound like a real calendar and signal that you're organized.

CONFIRM AND GIVE LANDMARK

Perfect. So I have you scheduled for [Day] at [Time] with me, [Your Name], at [Dealership Name]. We're located at [Address], the easiest landmark is [nearby landmark, e.g., right across from the HEB on South Main, or just past the Target on Route 31]. If you'd like, I can send you a pin drop by text right now so you have it on your phone.

The landmark is critical. An address alone means nothing if they don't know the area. Give them something they can picture. The pin-drop offer is a natural use of the text permission you already have.

CONFIRM NAME AND CLOSE

And I've got you as [Name]. Did I get that right? Great. I'll see you [Day] at [Time]. If anything comes up before then, feel free to call or text me directly at [Your Number].

I'm looking forward to it.

Repeat their name, confirm the appointment, and give them your direct number. Personal contact signals that you're accessible and takes some of the dealership-as-institution feeling out of it.

Script 2: Outbound Call Internet Lead or Previous Inquiry

Use when following up on a submitted form, an online inquiry, or a customer who came in previously but didn't purchase. Your goal is the same: information, connection, appointment.

OPENING

Hi, is this [Name]? Great, this is [Your Name] calling from [Dealership Name]. You [submitted an inquiry / came in last week / reached out about a vehicle], and I wanted to follow up personally. Did I catch you at a decent time?

Always ask if it's a good time. It shows respect and immediately sets you apart from robocalls and pushy follow-ups.

IF YES, CONTINUE

I appreciate that. I just wanted to make sure someone actually reached out to you, because I know it can feel like you submit a form and nobody follows up. I'd love to understand a little more about what you're looking for so we're ready for you when you come in.

Position yourself as the exception, not the rule. Most internet leads get called by a robot or a generic follow-up. Make it personal.

QUALIFY

Are you still looking for [vehicle type/vehicle they inquired about]? And what's your situation? Are you replacing something, adding a vehicle, or just starting to explore options?

HANDLE PRICE QUESTION

I completely understand wanting to know the numbers before you come in. That's smart. What I'd rather do is make sure I have the right vehicle ready for you and then go over everything together. I can get you real numbers when I know more about your situation. It'll save us both time.

SET APPOINTMENT

Here's what I'd suggest to get you scheduled for a time when I can focus on you specifically. I have [Day] at [Time] or [alternate]. Which works better?

CONFIRM

Perfect. [Day] at [Time] with me, [Your Name], at [Dealership Name] on [Address], right [landmark]. I'll send you a text confirmation with the address and a pin drop so you have it. What's the best number for that?

Even if you already have their number, confirming it shows attention to detail, and sending the pin drop immediately after the call turns the text permission into an immediate value.

Script 3: Follow-Up Call After Visit, No Purchase

Use within 24–48 hours of a customer who did not purchase visiting. This is one of the highest-value calls you can make and one of the most neglected.

OPENING

Hi [Name], this is [Your Name] from [Dealership Name]. I just wanted to reach out personally and say thank you for coming in [yesterday / earlier this week]. I really enjoyed talking with you, and I want to make sure I answered everything you needed.

No pressure. No, "so are you ready to buy?" Just a genuine thank you and a check-in. This call surprises most customers because most salespeople never make it.

CHECK IN

Did you have a chance to think about the [vehicle] any more? And is there anything I didn't cover that would help you feel more confident about the decision?

You're not pushing. You're offering. There's a significant difference, and customers feel it.

IF THEY'RE STILL CONSIDERING

That makes complete sense. I'd rather you feel good about it than rush any-thing. Can I ask what the one thing you're still working through is? Sometimes I can answer something that makes it a lot clearer.

Draw out the specific objection. Vague hesitation is hard to resolve. A specific concern gives you something to work with.

OFFER TO COME BACK IN

If it would help, I'd be happy to have you come back in and take another look or do another drive. No pressure at all, I want to make sure you have everything you need. I have [Day] at [Time] if that works.

IF THEY'RE NOT INTERESTED

I completely understand, and I appreciate you letting me know. If anything changes, or if you have a friend or family member looking for a vehicle, I'd love the opportunity to help them the same way. Would it be all right if I stayed in touch?

Plant the referral seed without making it the point of the call. Asking to stay in touch is low-pressure and keeps the door open.

Script 4: Appointment Reminder Text or Call

Send the day before the scheduled appointment. Text is preferred; it's less intrusive and more likely to be seen.

TEXT VERSION

Hi [Name], this is [Your Name] at [Dealership Name], just a friendly reminder that you're scheduled for tomorrow, [Day] at [Time]. We're at [Address], right [landmark]. Reply here if you need to reschedule or if you have any questions before you come in. Looking forward to seeing you.

Keep it short and practical. Include the landmark every time, don't assume they remember. Inviting a reply makes it feel like a two-way conversation, not a broadcast.

CALL VERSION

Hi [Name], this is [Your Name] from [Dealership Name]. I just wanted to give you a quick call to confirm we have you scheduled for [Day] at [Time]. We're right [landmark on Address]. Is that still a good time for you?

If they confirm, great. If they need to reschedule, offer two new times immediately. Don't let them hang up without a new appointment on the books.

IF THEY NEED TO RESCHEDULE

No problem at all, I want to make sure it works with your schedule. I have [new option 1] or [new option 2]. Which one works better?

Script 5: Missed Appointment

Use within an hour of a no-show. Keep it warm, not accusatory. Life happens; your job is to get them back on the calendar.

TEXT FIRST

Hi [Name], this is [Your Name] at [Dealership Name]. We had you scheduled for [Time] today and wanted to make sure everything is okay. No worries at all if something came up, I'd love to find a time that works better for you. I have [option 1] or [option 2] this week. Just reply here, and we'll get you set up.

Text before calling a no-show. It's less confrontational and more likely to get a response. The tone is concern, not frustration.

FOLLOW-UP CALL IF NO TEXT RESPONSE

Hi [Name], this is [Your Name] from [Dealership Name]. I just wanted to reach out personally. We had you down for [Time] today and wanted to make sure everything's all right. Suppose something came up, absolutely no problem. I'd love to get you rescheduled when the timing is better. I have [option 1] or [option 2], either one works?

Script 6: Voicemail

Keep it under 30 seconds. Voicemails that are too long get deleted before they finish. Give them one clear reason to call back.

STANDARD VOICEMAIL

Hi [Name], this is [Your Name] calling from [Dealership Name]. I'm following up on [the vehicle you inquired about / your visit earlier this week / your appointment], and I wanted to make sure I personally answered any questions you might have. You can reach me directly at [Your Number], which is [repeat number].

I look forward to hearing from you. Have a great day.

Say your number twice, speaking each time. Nothing is more frustrating than a voicemail from which you can't catch the number from. Saying it twice removes that friction completely.

VEHICLE-SPECIFIC VOICEMAIL

Hi [Name], this is [Your Name] at [Dealership Name]. I'm calling because the [year/make/model] you were interested in is still available, and I wanted to make sure you had the chance to see it before it moves. Please give me a call at [Your Number] [repeat number] or feel free to text me there. I'd love to get you in this week.

Creating mild urgency around a specific vehicle is legitimate when it's true. Don't manufacture urgency, but if the vehicle is popular or inventory is limited, say so.

Script 7: Text Message Scripts

Text is the most effective communication channel for most customers today. Always identify yourself and your dealership in every text; your number may not be in their contacts. Keep texts conversational and short.

FIRST CONTACT TEXT AFTER PERMISSION GRANTED

Hi [Name], this is [Your Name] from [Dealership Name]. Great talking with you. Here's our address and a pin drop so you have them for [Day] at [Time]. [Insert pin drop link]. Let me know if anything comes up or if you have any questions before you come in.

VEHICLE FOLLOW-UP TEXT

Hi [Name], [Your Name] at [Dealership Name]. Just wanted to follow up on the [vehicle] we talked about. It's still here, and I'd love to have you take another look. Are you free [Day] at [Time] or [alternate]?

APPOINTMENT REMINDER TEXT

Hi [Name], a reminder from [Your Name] at [Dealership Name]: you're scheduled for tomorrow at [Time]. Right [landmark on Address]. Reply if you need anything. See you then.

DAY-OF CHECK-IN TEXT

Good [morning/afternoon] [Name] [Your Name] here at [Dealership Name]. Looking forward to seeing you at [Time] today. I'll have everything ready for you when you arrive.

A day-of text makes the customer feel expected and prepared. It also reduces no-shows because they know someone is specifically waiting for them.

AFTER VISIT NO PURCHASE

Hi [Name], [Your Name] from [Dealership Name]. Really glad you came in today. If anything comes up or you have questions, don't hesitate to reach out. The [vehicle] will be here. Just let me know if you'd like to come back for another look.

Script 8: Objection Handling

Remember: respond, don't answer. An answer gives them a specific number or commitment before you have enough information. A response acknowledges the concern, explains why you can't answer it yet, and moves toward the appointment.

OBJECTION: "HOW MUCH IS THE CAR?"

That's going to depend on a few things, whether you have a trade, any down payment, and how you want to structure the financing. I want to give you accurate numbers, not a rough estimate that might not apply to your situation. The best way to do that is to get you in so we can look at the whole picture together. I can have everything ready for you. I have [Day] at [Time] or [alternate], which works better?

OBJECTION: "WHAT ARE MY PAYMENTS GOING TO BE?"

Payments will be based on your credit, your down payment, the vehicle, and the term length. There are a few moving parts. What I can tell you is that my job is to get you to a payment that works for your budget. The only way I can do that accurately is to sit down with you. Can we get you in at [Day/Time] so we can put together some real numbers?

OBJECTION: "WHAT WILL YOU GIVE ME FOR MY TRADE?"

That's going to be determined by our appraisal team based on the mileage, condition, and current market, and I want to make sure you get every dollar it's worth. The fastest way to find that out is to bring it in. When can you come by? I have [Day] at [Time] if that works.

OBJECTION: "I NEED TO THINK ABOUT IT"

I completely understand this is a significant decision, and I'd never want you to rush it. Can I ask what specifically you'd like to think over? Sometimes there's something I can answer right now that makes the decision a lot clearer.

Move vague hesitation to a specific concern. Vague hesitation can't be resolved. A specific concern can.

OBJECTION: "I'M JUST SHOPPING AROUND"

That's smart, it makes sense to look at your options. Can I ask what you're comparing? I want to make sure that when you compare, you're looking at similar vehicles and terms so it's a fair comparison. And if I can save you some time by having everything ready when you come in, I'd love to. I have [Day] at [Time], or [alternate]. Even a quick visit might save you a few stops.

OBJECTION: "I NEED TO TALK TO MY SPOUSE"

Of course, these are decisions you want to make together. What do you think your spouse is going to want to know most? Maybe I can answer that right now so you can go home with the full picture. And if it would be easier, you're both welcome to come in together I can have everything ready for both of you. I have [Day] at [Time] if that works.

Offer to include the spouse rather than treating it as an obstacle. Getting both decision-makers in front of you at the same time is almost always better than one person relaying information to another.

OBJECTION: "THE PAYMENT IS TOO HIGH"

I hear you, nobody wants to feel stretched on a payment. Can I ask whether it is higher than you expected, or higher than you can actually manage each month? Because those are two different things, and I'd like to make sure I understand which one we're working with.

Separate the two possible meanings before responding. The solution for "higher than expected" is different from the solution for "higher than my budget." Don't guess which one it is.

OBJECTION: "I'M NOT COMING IN UNLESS YOU GIVE ME A PRICE FIRST"

I completely respect that, and I want to be straight with you, the reason I can't give you an accurate price over the phone is that I don't have enough information yet. If I give you a number now and it's off when you get here, that's worse than not having a number at all. What I can promise you is that when you come in, I'll have real numbers ready, and we won't waste your time. Even thirty minutes could give you everything you need to make a decision. I have [Day] at [Time]. Would that work?

Quick Reference: Appointment Setting Rules

Always use quarter-hour time slots.

"I have an opening at 2:15 or Thursday at 10:45" sounds like a real calendar. Round numbers ("2:00 or 4:00") sound like placeholders. Quarter-hour times signal organization and that you're treating their appointment seriously.

Always give them two options.

"Would [Time 1] or [Time 2] work better for you?" Both options are a yes. You're giving them a choice, not asking an open question that could lead to "neither."

Always give a landmark.

An address means nothing if they don't know the area. Give them something they can picture: "right across from the HEB on South Main" or "just past the Home Depot on Route 31." Always follow up with a pin drop by text.

Always collect name, phone number, and email address.

All three. Every time. A customer without contact information is a lead you can't follow up on.

Always ask permission to text.

Explain why: you can send a pin drop, directions, vehicle information, and reminders. Most customers prefer text to phone calls. Getting permission turns texting into a service instead of an intrusion.

Always confirm everything before ending the call.

Name, day, time, your name, dealership name, address, landmark. Say it all back to them. A customer who hears their appointment confirmed in full is far less likely to no-show.

Full digital versions of these scripts, additional objection handling scenarios, and updates as the industry evolves are available to readers of this book at the website listed in the back matter. Enter your email to receive the complete script library and access to the full Car Sales Survival Series.

KEY TAKEAWAYS

Every chapter of this book ended with a rule. Here they are collected in one place, a quick-reference summary of the principles that matter most.

Chapter 1: The Reality of the Car Business

"The car business will give you everything you're willing to earn. It won't give you anything you're not."

Chapter 2: Before You Walk Out That Door

"Manage your money before it manages you. Know your floor, bank the difference, and take your vacation in January."

Chapter 3: The Disneyland Principle

"The moment you step onto that lot, you're on stage. The character you play is the best version of yourself. Stay in character."

Chapter 4: Dancing the Waltz

"The steps are the dance. Follow the sequence every time, and the sale flows. Skip a step, and you're flailing on the floor."

Chapter 5: The Four Types of Buyers

"Know what your customer cares about, and sell to that. Everything else is just noise."

Chapter 6: The Meet and Greet

"The meet and greet starts the moment they see you. From that instant, you are either building trust or destroying it. Make sure you're doing it on purpose."

Chapter 7: Set on a Vehicle in Stock

"Ask more than you talk. The customer will tell you exactly how to sell them if you're willing to listen."

Chapter 8: Demo All Features and the Test Drive

"Never ask if they want to test drive the car. Lead them to it. The experience of being in the vehicle is what converts interest into a decision."

Chapter 9: Establishing the Price

"Numbers on your seat, commitment on paper. You can't present a deal to the desk until the customer has made a move. Get the initial. Ask for the deposit if required. Then go fight for them."

Chapter 10: Presenting to the Desk

"Know what you're walking into before you walk into the desk. Context closes deals. Numbers alone don't."

Chapter 11: Closing the Sale

"If you've done the work, you've earned the right to ask. Ask directly, stop talking, and let the customer say yes."

Chapter 12: Follow Up

"The sale ends when the customer drives away. The relationship starts there. Take care of the relationship, and the sales take care of themselves."

Chapter 13: CRM

"Your CRM is your customer bank. What you put in is what you get out. Fill it in completely, work it every day, and let the tools handle the consistency while you handle the connection."

Chapter 14: Scripts

"Don't read the script. Own it. Translate it into your voice, practice it until it's automatic, and use it every time without exception."

Chapter 15: Customer One

"The customer doesn't know your process. They only know how it felt. Every person in the building shapes that feeling. Make sure yours is the right one."

Chapter 16: The Psychology of the Customer

"Understand the person before you try to sell them the car. Everything else flows from that."

Chapter 17: What Annoys Me About Salespeople

"Be the salesperson you'd want to buy from. Everything else follows from that."

Chapter 18: Moving Up

"Moving up is not given. It's built deal by deal, role by role, year by year. Stay ready, stay visible, and create your own path when the obvious one is closed."

Chapter 19: Buy Here Pay Here

"Same respect. Different rules. BHPH is not a lesser version of the car business. It's a more complex one."

Also Available

The Complete Car Sales Survival Guide is the flagship of The Car Sales Survival Series, a growing collection of focused micro-books that go deep into one specific sales skill.

Each book in the series is designed to stand alone as a focused training resource. Use them individually for targeted development, or as a complete system for onboarding new sales staff. Bulk orders are available for dealerships and sales organizations.

The Meet and Greet Playbook

How to Make Powerful First Impressions with Customers, Clients, and Guests

The First 60 Seconds in Car Sales

A Proven Meet and Greet System to Build Trust and Start More Conversations

How to Handle "I'm Just Looking" in Car Sales

A Simple System to Turn Brush-Offs into Productive Conversations

Body Language in Car Sales

How Posture, Eye Contact, and Presence Build Customer Trust

Greeting Customers on the Lot

How to Approach Buyers Without Pressure

The Ten-Second Rule in Car Sales

Why First Impressions Determine Whether Customers Stay or Leave

The Car Sales Conversation Starter Guide

How to Begin Natural Conversations That Lead to Sales

Car Sales Confidence for New Salespeople

How to Approach Customers Without Fear or Hesitation

Common Car Sales Greeting Mistakes

What Drives Customers Away in the First Minute

The First Five Minutes With a Car Buyer

How to Transition from Greeting to Conversation and Move Toward the Sale

Additional titles in the series are in development, including dedicated books on the buy-here, pay-here sales process, portfolio management, and underwriting.

Order individual copies or inquire about bulk pricing:

www.bedrockheritagepublishing.com

info@bedrockheritagepublishing.com

www.carsalessurvivalseries.com

WORK WITH BRUCE

This book is a starting point. For salespeople and teams who want to go deeper, working through the material personally, applying it to their specific situation, and building the habits that make it stick, Bruce offers individual and group sessions through Life Guidance Consulting LLC.

One-on-One Coaching

Individual sessions for salespeople at any stage of their career. Whether you're in your first ninety days on the floor or you've been selling for years and want to break through a plateau, one-on-one coaching gives you direct access to thirty-five years of real-world experience applied specifically to your situation, your dealership, and your goals.

Group Training Sessions

Group sessions for sales teams working through The Complete Car Sales Survival Guide or The Car Sales Survival Series together. Ideal for dealership onboarding, team development, and ongoing skills training. Sessions are practical, direct, and built around real scenarios from the sales floor, not theory.

Bulk Book Orders

Dealerships and sales organizations interested in using The Complete Car Sales Survival Guide or The Car Sales Survival Series as structured onboarding or training materials can inquire about bulk pricing and customized packages.

Life Guidance Consulting LLC
www.lifeguidanceconsulting.com

bruce@lifeguidanceconsulting.com

For book orders and publishing inquiries:

www.bedrockheritagepublishing.com

info@bedrockheritagepublishing.com

About the Author

Bruce Huddleston spent thirty-five years in the automotive industry, working every level of the business from showroom floor salesperson to finance manager, sales manager, used car manager, and general manager. His career included new-car franchise dealerships, independent used-car operations, and a decade in buy-here, pay-here, giving him a breadth of experience that few in the industry can match.

He began as a high school dropout who needed a job and ended up discovering a profession. He ended as a veteran who had trained hundreds of salespeople, managed multiple departments, and built a reputation for straight talk in an industry that doesn't always reward it.

Since retiring, Bruce has opened a life coaching practice, assists his wife with her mental health therapy practice, and operates Bedrock Heritage Publishing, a division of Life Guidance Consulting LLC, where he writes practical guides for sales professionals across multiple industries.

The Complete Car Sales Survival Guide is his flagship work. The Car Sales Survival Series, a collection of focused microbooks on specific sales skills, is built on the same foundation of real experience, honest insight, and zero tolerance for the kind of nonsense that gives sales a bad name.

He lives in Tyler, Texas.

www.lifeguidanceconsulting.com
www.bedrockheritagepublishing.com

A Quick Favor

If The Complete Car Sales Survival Guide gave you something useful, a technique that landed, a story that stuck, a framework that helped you close a deal you might have lost, the single best thing you can do to help other salespeople find it is leave an honest review on Amazon.
It takes about two minutes. It makes a real difference to how the book gets discovered. And it helps the next new salesperson who needs this information actually find it.

You can simply scan the QR code below

https://www.amazon.com/review/create-review/?asin=1972179411

Thank you for reading. Now sell some cars.

Bruce Huddleston